A Year of Birding Nantucket

Volume Three

By Kenneth Turner Blackshaw

Illustrations by George C. West

Published by: Booksurge Publishing

Order at web address:
http://k-blackshaw.nstemp.com/AYBN3/AYBN3.htm

Or by mail at: BookSurge Publishing
7290-B Investment Dr
N. Charleston, SC 29418

Telephone: (866) 308-6235 ext. 6

Library of Congress Cataloging in Publication Data

Blackshaw, Kenneth T. (Kenneth Turner)
A Year of Birding Nantucket (Volume Three)

ISBN – 1-4196-8000-5   Manufactured in the USA

First Edition, Volume Three

Cover Design: Composite designed by George C. West from background photo by Kenneth Turner Blackshaw with original artwork superimposed.

Table of Contents

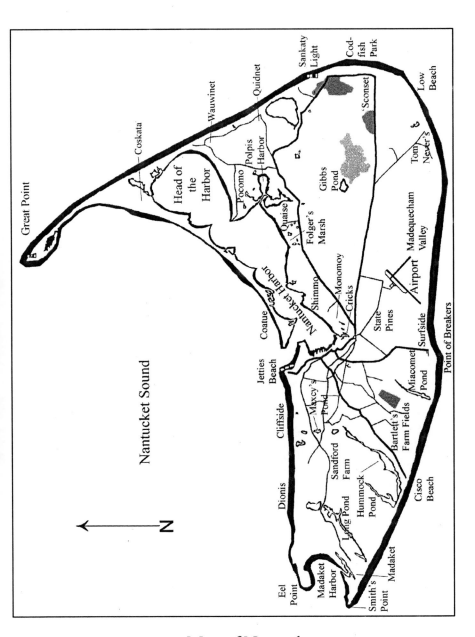

Map of Nantucket

Foreword

Birds become a source of intense fascination to some people, but it is rare in young children. Ken Blackshaw and I have this fascination in common – both natives of Massachusetts, becoming entranced with bird identification and behavior in grammar school, and maintaining that interest throughout life. This parallel in our life-paths means that I can easily understand Ken's desire to continue to study, learn, explore, and write about birds wherever he lives. For those lucky enough to live on or visit Nantucket Island, Ken lives there and does not hesitate to take every chance possible to keep track of the local birds, discover the unexpected strays, and let you, the reader, in on his research and knowledge of each species he comes across.

Ken and I have been working together for almost 10 years now – where he does the writing and I do the illustrations. My own bird-related writing has been mostly in scientific journals and more recently in guide books to Alaskan birds. But doing illustrations for Nantucket birds is no different from drawing Alaskan birds and I have enjoyed coming up with sketches that fit his weekly columns such as those you find in this third volume of birds he writes about so well – and that are found on Nantucket Island. The sketches in this volume are more advanced in style and print than those in volumes one and two. You will see that many are in shades of gray rather than just black and white, and that the drawings "hold together" better than earlier as the printer now uses a much finer screen to convert the gray tones to tiny distributed black dots called "half tones."

Writing for the general public is much more difficult than writing for the scientific community or for birders who "have to read" your text in order to find birds. Ken has the ability to hold your attention as you become involved with each species he writes about. You want to read on to the next account and learn about how this species relates to history of the island, where it resides and why, how it interacts with other species and with humans on the island, and how you can learn to identify it by its habits, its calls, its shape and size, and its plumage colors. I suspect that many readers have become birders – maybe not as ardent as Ken or I – at least at first – but interested enough to pick up a pair of binoculars and wander the island in search of some of the species Ken has described for you in books such as this one.

Becoming a birder is more often than not a step to becoming a conservationist. Some folks go at it backwards – being concerned with a vanishing habitat and then noticing that birds there have become fewer over time. There is nothing wrong with being a birder conservationist as this will lead you towards assisting landowners, whether governmental or private, in maintaining all or part of their land to assure that the next human generation will be able to see the birds you now enjoy. This is an educational process and should not be an adversarial one. Birds are not only important to many phases of our economy such as plant pollinators, noxious insect predators, plant distributors (via seeds), scavengers, and food (hunting), but also to our emotional and psychic well-being. Can you imagine a world without the flight, color, and song of birds in your backyard? We can't. By being an active birder conservationist, you can help prevent habitat loss that is the chief reason for the decline of birds in the world. Books such as this one and others written by Ken Blackshaw will assist in the conservation process by raising the public awareness and collective conscience about the value of birds in our lives.

George C. West, Green Valley, Arizona

Acknowledgments

There are many people and institutions to thank when I think about how this book was written.

First there are people who started me on my avian journey over half a century ago – my Mom, Merle Turner Blackshaw Orleans, and my lifelong mentor, Edith Folger Andrews. Having an island institution like the Maria Mitchell Association provided an atmosphere that brought science to life, with scientific links and inspiration for my birding beginnings, starting with the mounted bird specimens in the Hinchman House.

People with whom I've birded over the years, Dr. Sheldon Severinghaus in Taiwan, Terry Moore and Giff Beaton in Georgia, Mary Dommermuth and Dave Smith down in Florida, and the wonderful Nantucket birders including Edith Andrews, Edie Ray, Marcia Aguiar, Lee Morgan, Dr. Bob Kennedy, and most recently, Vernon Laux, have all made contributions to my enjoyment, appreciation, and understanding of birds.

People who have read this text and greatly improved it include Dr. George C. West, Edith Andrews, Dr. Martin Horowitz, and Lee Morgan. My wife, Cynthia Blackshaw, while not an enthusiastic birder, is nonetheless a 'captive' reader who gets an opportunity every week to improve my work.

I'm very pleased that the Arizona to Nantucket partnership continues with my bird artist, Dr. George C. West. Initially the illustrator for *Bike Birding Nantucket,* and then with Volume One and Two in this series, George continues to come through with the illustrations I need to help bring my words to life.

I'd also like to thank Steve Sheppard, Sports Editor, and Don Costanzo, Owner and Publisher of *The Nantucket Independent* newspaper for their continued confidence and support giving my work prominent display every week. I am frequently reinforced by positive comments from readers and that helps to jump-start me every Tuesday morning to craft another column.

Books used regularly include my 24 volume set of Arthur Cleveland Bent's *Life Histories of North American Birds*, now available on-line; Ernest A. Choate's *The Dictionary of American Bird Names*; all of Roger Tory Peterson's field guides, Eastern, Western, and Britain and Europe; *The Birds of Nantucket,* by Ludlow Griscom and Edith V. Folger; *The Sibley Guide to Birds,* by David Allen Sibley; and an old favorite set of guides by Richard H. Pough from the early 1950s, *The Audubon Land, Water and Western Bird Guides.*

My web browser is always cooking in the background of my writing screen. Many searches start with Google, but I also regularly use http://www.birdzilla.com, and I'm a real fan of the on-line encyclopedia, Wikipedia.

All the writing and formatting has been done using Microsoft Word on an IBM compatible PC. Word corrects my atrocious spelling, watches my syntax, and hands me synonyms from its thesaurus as needed. My first books were done on paper with an old Royal typewriter. I'd hate to go back to that era again.

Introduction

This is the third in a series of books that take a weekly snapshot of what it's like to be a bird watcher on Nantucket Island. We start at the beginning of October and go through the seasons. These articles were originally published in the *Nantucket Independent* newspaper. If you enjoy reading these bird stories you will also enjoy Volumes One and Two, available at all of Nantucket's bookstores.

With just a few exceptions, these are birds you might find on our island in any year. So, depending when you read this, you can page through to an article around that date and find out about a bird that is doing something interesting.

Most of Nantucket's birds are here for only part of the year. Many of our summer birds winter in Central or South America. Many of our winter birds are high in the Arctic during the summer. Then there are vagrant birds that visit from the far west or even from across the Atlantic. As Roger Tory Peterson said, "Birds have wings and they use them."

As you read through these essays, you experience all the seasons of island life, for the birds reflect the essence of these months as much as the harbor ice in the winter and the waves of tourists in the summer.

Writing weekly columns like this is an adventure. Birds have always grasped my imagination and attention. My mentor, Edith Folger Andrews comments about me, "He was born with birds in his eyes." She is so correct, and I might add, "with their songs in my ears."

People ask, "Do you go birding every day?" And the answer is, "Yes!" But birding can be more pervasive than that. I am distracted even from sleep by a birdcall, like the cry of a Common Loon flying over the house at 5:30 a.m. I have butchered playing easy bridge hands when a Crested Flycatcher calls from the yard. Even as I type this, a House Finch and a Northern Cardinal are sparring on the feeder outside my window and there goes my train of thought.

As I research these flying wonders I find out about unfamiliar or exotic parts of the world, places like Ungava and Slavonia. I read about flocks of birds that darken the sky and bird's nests that would fill a whole wagon. I am reminded how humans have wiped out whole species by shooting, poisoning or depriving them of their homes. So, the articles are not just descriptive of what a bird may look like, they touch on history, geography, and also the way things once were on this special island.

Nantucket and its birds have evolved significantly over my 50 plus years of study. Wind and waves have chopped the island into pieces at both ends and then reconnected it. Climate change is bringing us species that we used to travel south to observe. Some species have recovered from over-hunting. Others are gone due to habitat loss associated with our island's development. Each species' story weaves a thread into the changing fabric that cloaks this special 15 by four-mile drift of sand in the Atlantic.

So no matter when you start reading, there is birding drama and amazement here for you to enjoy. If you are not already a birder maybe something you'll read will encourage you to pick up a pair of binoculars and look at one of your feathered neighbors. Observe what it is doing and then ask yourself, "Why is it doing that?" Birds are all around us and if you start watching them your life will become richer indeed.

October 7 – Winter's-a-comin' and the

Long Johns are Here!

It's a lovely Nantucket autumn morning out on the Polpis Road heading in from 'Sconset. The cut off to Hoick's Hollow is just behind us as we crest the little rise bringing Sesachacha Pond into view. Pulling into the little turn off on the right, we can see three or four large birds spaced well apart on the far shore. They look dark, standing tall and erect, motionless like sentinels. Our first guess is they are Great Blue Herons and a binocular view quickly confirms the supposition.

This is one of the 'non-garden' birds that almost everyone knows. Unfortunately people call them 'cranes,' which they are not, but at least they notice them.

Since Great Blue Herons are so hard to miss, they have many nicknames, the 'Big Cranky,' because of their croaking call, the 'Blue Crane' and yes -- 'Long John.' Its Latin name *Ardea herodias,* is redundant, meaning "heron-heron," one word coming from Latin, the other, Greek.

This season is the best one for viewing this striking bird on Nantucket. Long Johns are common all over North America even up into

Canada but rare here in July and August. Only non-nesting birds remain at that season. But now the northern part of the population is headed south and lots of people are seeing these dignified-looking birds.

Great Blue Herons are large, standing over three feet tall with almost a six foot wingspan and weighing as much as eight pounds. They are gray above, perhaps slate blue in good light, darker underneath, and have a lighter neck with a white stripe down the front. There is a black line through the eye extending to plumes at the back of the head. The rather dagger-like beak is yellow at the base, fading to black at the tip.

In flight they are quite impressive, flying on slow wing beats with their long legs trailing behind. Most of the time, their neck is tucked back against the body in flight, a good way to tell them from a Sandhill Crane that flies with the neck extended.

There are 60 species of herons worldwide. In Eurasia, the Gray Heron is a close relative, looking very similar to our Great Blue. In southern Florida there is a 'morph' of this species that is totally white. At one time known as the Great White Heron, it is now considered just a variant. If you visit the keys, try and check this critter out since it may be split out again in the future.

Most often you see these big birds at the edge of a pond or wading therein. Their diet is mostly fish, but they are opportunistic in their feeding habits. One heron's stomach was found to be full of field mice! Sometimes they will pose, motionless, waiting for a fish to approach, other times they stalk, hunched forward, lashing out to catch an unwary prey. Audubon saw one spear a fish that was too large and off it went, dragging the hapless heron both above and below the water before the bird could disengage.

Great Blue Herons don't nest here, or even on the Cape. Perhaps there aren't enough of the tall trees they like, or there is too much predation from the gulls. Almost no creature will attack a full-grown 'Long John,' but the nestlings and eggs are easier targets.

Their mating activities are spectacular and Audubon wrote extensively about them, describing how 40 or more would gather on a sandbar and then immense sword fights would break out amongst the males deciding who would get to mate with the waiting females. By the way, outwardly the sexes look the same to us, but the herons know who is who.

After all the swordplay, the chosen couples retire to nest for the summer and peace again reigns. Great Blue Herons like to nest high in trees, often choosing tall dead deciduous trees that may hold a dozen of the three foot nests. Usually there are four eggs and both parents share the 28-day incubation period.

Arthur Cleveland Bent describes the young as "far from attractive … at first they are feeble and helpless, but later on they are awkward, ungainly, and pugnacious." Know any children like this?

They are fed a regurgitated slurry of fish at first and whole fish later. When visiting a rookery the overall effect of vast amounts of droppings and fish residue makes the use of an umbrella and nose clips mandatory.

You can spot a young Great Blue by its black rather than white forehead. They also lack the black marks at the fold of the wing. Studies have shown that two thirds of the chicks don't make it past their first year but once they are grown, 10 or 15 years in the wild is not unusual.

Here on Nantucket this stately creature stays with us as long as there is open water in which to fish. We get them on most all of our Christmas Bird Counts and have had over 50 of them several times. In addition to Sesachacha, look across Folger's Marsh, the Cricks, or the salt marshes at Eel Point. If you see a huge bird flying by with its landing gear extending behind, you are probably seeing a Long John.

October 14 – Bright Eyes

"Bright-eyes!" was a sarcastic nickname that dogged me during my tortured youth. But it is also the key to distinguishing this week's bird.

Here is a bird that tantalized me for years. There it was in my Peterson Guide, poised above the grackles, just on the next page from the Red-wings. I would read tales of thousands of these birds in eastern Massachusetts during migration and was mystified by Griscom and Folger's comment that there was only a single record for Nantucket and that back in 1925.

I'm writing about the Rusty Blackbird, a bird now thought of as an indicator of the relative health of the boreal forests of Canada for this is where most of them spend their summers and raise their families.

Like most beginning birders I was very anxious to add new birds to my list and it seemed like I was seeing Rusty Blackbirds every fall, all over the place! The problem is that of course *I wasn't*. But here is a test for most fledgling birdwatchers – Red-winged Blackbirds and Rusties.

You see, Red-winged Blackbirds don't all have red wings. And every 'rusty' blackbird is not a Rusty Blackbird. It's enough to make you throw up your hands and take up Parcheesi for a hobby. But think about 'bright eyes.'

Let's discuss what a Rusty should look like. First of all, it is blackbird-sized. That is, just a little smaller than a robin, but bigger than a sparrow. It has a medium-length tail, not long like a grackle's or stubby like a starling's. In the spring and summer, they are black and glossy, like little grackles. But the time to look for them here is in the fall and that's when the rustiness sets in. Rusty Blackbirds are only rusty in the fall and winter.

But at that season there are a huge number of 'teen-aged' and winter-plumaged Red-wings. These birds are the right size, and have rusty edges on their feathers, and could easily excite the new birder looking for a Rusty. But they lack one key factor, the title of this article. Their eyes are dark. Rusty Blackbirds of both sexes have very pale eyes. Particularly in the females, they are set against a dark background and seem to jump out at you, and they are the key to knowing you are looking at a Rusty Blackbird.

This species' belongs to the scientific genus *Euphagus* that strangely enough means "good to eat." Now this makes us think of the nursery rhyme about "Four and twenty blackbirds baked in a pie." But alas those were European Blackbirds that are thrushes, closely related to our American Robin. We'll just have to guess that the eminent ornithologist, John Cassin, may have tasted their flesh and remembered that when he named them.

Rusty Blackbirds travel through the central and eastern U.S. twice each year on their way to and from their north woods summer home. They breed as far north as they can find trees, showing a preference for fresh water. Scientists wanting to study their home life must flounder through swamps and bogs, and brave black flies, gnats, and mosquitoes, generally far from civilization.

Dr. Charles W. Townsend described their mating activities as follows, "The courtship of this bird, if such it may be called, is produced with apparently great effort, wide open bill and spread tail, resulting in a series of squeaking notes suggestive of an unoiled windmill." They don't make the birding hit parade with their singing ability.

Strangely this species is in decline and the sight of more than a few Rusty Blackbirds can cause excitement amongst birdwatchers. Although regularly viewed by the thousands near the turn of the 20th century, this species is now on the American Bird Conservancy list of Threatened or Declining Species. Our National Zoo's Migratory Bird Center featured them recently as the "Troubled Blackbird of the Bog."

We're guessing the reason is breeding habitat loss. Even though this species nests from Newfoundland to Alaska, the clear cutting of forests can threaten their numbers. But the problem may be more pervasive and insidious. Our boreal forests are also being attacked by climatological effects related to acid rain. Also, during the winter, Rusties like to gather into huge communal roosts often viewed as a health hazard and are sprayed with pesticide.

On Nantucket, we list them as rare from mid-September until the end of December, and also in March and April when they are harder to identify. Occasionally we get them on our Christmas Bird Counts. At this season, if you see a 'rusty' blackbird, see if you can pick out its bright eyes. If so, you have a true Rusty!

October 21 – The American Kestrel

My eyes followed the lure as it arced high in the crystal blue Colorado sky, then circled down past Ponderosa Pines, the faces and blue uniforms of several Air Force Academy Cadets, the aluminum spires of the Academy Chapel and then back up into the heavens again.

My next awareness was the sound of a faint jingling bell rapidly growing louder. The falconer swung the lure out in front of him, tantalizingly balancing centrifugal force with gravity before swiftly jerking it back past us both. The jingling reached a crescendo as a multicolored ball of feathers hurtled past – eyes – I remember those eyes, filled with fire and spirit, visible just for a millisecond. Then the pitch of the bells dropped as the sound tapered off.

I had seen many American Kestrels over the years but had never dreamed of training them for falconry. Although they are marvelous creatures, what hunter would keep a bird that would only catch grasshoppers and mice for him? This one was used to train the cadets in handling falcons before moving up to the larger hawks, and finally to the wonderful white-phase Gyrfalcon, Baffin, the official mascot.

What a thrill to see the resplendent little falcon catch the bait on the next pass and then perch murderously on the falconer's glove, ravenously tearing apart the chicken meat tied to the lure.

I had been used to seeing this exercise done with the big brown Prairie Falcons, more massive, but not much faster than this winged mite, but the panoply of colors this tiny raptor gave off was breathtaking. This was a male American Kestrel, *Falco sparverius*, at its best.

Back when I learned my birds we called them 'sparrow hawks,' actually the basis for *sparverius*. There were these, then 'pigeon hawks,' and finally 'duck hawks,' now Merlins and Peregrines. These were the three falcons to be learned. We could see the huge Gyrfalcons in our bird guides but never thought to actual find one.

Another tenet to be memorized was that "All falcons are hawks, but not all hawks are falcons." The raptor or hawk family includes eagles, buteos, accipiters, kites, *and* falcons. But it is the falcon that most captures the imagination, because with its pointed wings and tail, their mastery of the air truly quickens the heart of the observer.

So the Kestrel is a falcon and the smallest one you're likely to see. A male falcon is called a tiercel, meaning one-third smaller. In all raptors the female is a noticeably bigger bird. So a boy Kestrel runs nine inches long and a girl can be a foot – robin or jay sized. But there the similarity ends. You'll never see a Kestrel on your front lawn, unless it is clutching a robin.

Kestrels are usually seen in the air, or perched on a post, hunting. They sit erectly, occasionally flicking their tail. In flight they often hover into the wind on rapidly beating wings. Their whistled cry "killy-killy-killy" carries a long way. Both Peterson and Sibley show the male Kestrel to be a stunningly pretty bird. The back is rufous brown, barred with black, as is the tail with a dark band near the end. The wings are slate blue, and the breast, white below blending to a creamy orange with spots on the flanks. The head shows a black teardrop, a white sideburn, and then a pair of 'false eyes' at the back. The female is similar but lacks the blue-gray on the wings.

Kestrels nest over most of the U.S. and southern Canada. They are unique amongst birds of prey in that they are hole nesters. A box put up for a flicker (woodpecker) might be used by a Kestrel. They usually lay four or five eggs and can live more than 10 years in the wild. Their diet is insects, birds, mammals, reptiles, and amphibians. Vegetarians need not apply.

Sadly, like so many animals at the top of the food chain, Kestrels are not doing well. We remember them as birds we would often see on Nantucket, even nesting. Now they seem to only show up in migration and into early winter. Until the mid-80s we would typically get 10 or more on a Christmas Bird Count but this has dwindled to one or two, and not every year.

From mid-September on through October is the best time to see a Kestrel on Nantucket. Usually they are in passage, seen along the south shore, flying westward across the island. These are often hatch-year birds, finding their way south for the first time. If you see a bird hovering into the wind on pointed wing-tips, listen for the 'killy-killy-killy' call and you have yourself a Kestrel.

October 28 – The Greyhound of Ducks

Picture a greyhound in your mind, not galloping along but rather just standing. Think of the elegant lines, the subtle brown coloration, and the overall demeanor of the animal.

Now think about a duck. Unfortunately the first image that comes to mind nowadays is the Aflac duck. There it is, white and a bit dumpy and awkward. Now morph it into a greyhound duck. Take the bill and stretch out the neck. Trim down the body. Grab the tail and stretch it out to a point. Make it greyhound colored – grays and soft browns and have it float gracefully in the water, taller and more slender than the other ducks. Now you have created the subject of this week's column – the Northern Pintail.

Here is a duck that, because its range is circumpolar, grasps the attention and imagination of sportsmen around the world. Since they are never really common it is always a treat to find them. I remember being surprised to see one amongst the Spot-billed Ducks on a flooded rice paddy on another island – Taiwan.

The Northern Pintail was almost unknown on Nantucket when Griscom and Folger collected our bird records in the late 40s. Now we find them here in small numbers through the winter as long as there is open fresh water.

When birders learn about ducks, they learn there are two major classes, dabblers and divers. Divers plunge and swim under the water to feed whereas dabblers just tip forward to grab what they can reach from the bottom. Pintails are dabblers.

As you drive out along Miacomet Pond Road, stop where you see ducks tipping and feeding in the water. These are mostly Mallards and American Wigeons, but among them look for those that are taller, slimmer, like elegant figure skaters amidst the masses. This profile is your first clue that pintails may be part of the group, particularly if they are in deeper water since their longer necks give them an advantage here.

It's important to be able to recognize the shape since many of the pintails we see are females and being brown, are easily confused with female mallards and black ducks. But their slim shape coupled with a trim charcoal gray bill and an unmarked head distinguish them.

Of course the drake Northern Pintail is an easy call. The shape gives one the feeling they are somewhere between a duck and a swan. The head is chocolate brown with a white strip vertically up the neck from a white breast. Most of the body is pearl gray, with cream, then black at the rear extending to the long and delicately pointed tail feathers. These feathers are the basis for the bird's Latin name, *Anas acuta,* literally 'sharp' duck.

Like most dabblers, pintails take flight easily, springing straight into the air. This is contrasted with diving ducks like scaup and scoters that have to run across the water into the wind before becoming airborne. In flight, Northern Pintails tend to travel in lines rather then compact flocks, again, their long thin wings and stretched profile make them look different.

Hunters feel they are faster than other ducks, approaching 90 miles per hour at times, and consider them a worthy adversary with excellent 'table' qualities. If you are an animal, excellent table qualities don't bode well for you – much like that deer in the 'Far Side' cartoon with the bulls-eye birthmark on its flank.

Despite this, Northern Pintails are holding their own. In North America they nest in the Arctic from Alaska to Hudson Bay, often being the first to arrive in this hostile environment in early May when the snow is still deep. The drakes court dramatically, arching their long necks into a curve so beak rests on chest, at the same time holding the delicate 'pin' tail vertically behind. Typically the hens lay seven to 10 eggs in a simple ground nest.

We know more about game bird longevity than other types of birds since hunters are good about turning bands into the Fish and Wildlife service. One pintail lived over 21 years in the wild, a testament to their wiliness. They are famous for flying extremely high over a marsh and then descending almost vertically to land in order to avoid gunshots.

Look for these waterfowl greyhounds from now through April as long as the ponds don't freeze up. We have a found a few on every Christmas Bird Count since 1976. Other places to look are in Long Pond near Massasoit Bridge and in the duck pond at Consue Springs.

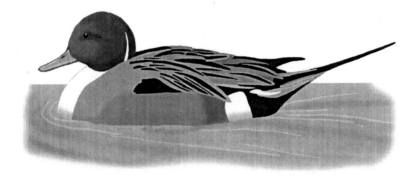

November 4 – As Red as You Can Get!

Here's a bird that's always stood out in my mind. The pictures in my Peterson Guide were so striking. And I still remember my initial sighting, here on Nantucket, 50 years ago.

It was a gray and windy day in late October and I was riding my bike back toward town from 'Sconset along the Polpis Road. I was just past the golf links when a medium-sized bird flew by me with a sort of roller-coaster flight. As it flew by it showed a white 'tee' pattern on the back and lower wing before clamping itself to the side of a phone pole. That was enough. We have nothing else that looks like that. I didn't even need to see the body part it was named for. This was a Red-headed Woodpecker.

You never know how seeing a bird will affect other people. Years later living near Atlanta, this species was common and would feast on the sunflower seeds in our tube feeder. This is a difficult posture for a woodpecker to feed but it seems these seeds have a bit of an addictive quality.

My wife really is not a birder but when she spotted this one, the red just knocked her eye out. Seeing the head she exclaimed, "Oh my God, look at that color!" We have many discussions on colors, stemming from the deluxe Crayola set she had as a child. For instance, a Northern Cardinal is more of a tomato red. The Red-headed Woodpecker is the only one she proclaims as true red!

Of course, people are always telling me they are seeing Red-headed Woodpeckers. That's because many kinds of woodpeckers show at least some red on their head. A Downy Woodpecker has a little checker of red at the back. A Red-bellied Woodpecker's head is red from their forehead across the top to the nape of the neck. I'll just let you imagine what a Yellow-bellied Sapsucker looks like.

Unfortunately, a true Red-headed Woodpecker is an unusual find on Nantucket. And to make matters worse, not all of them have red heads. Alas, my first one, my LIFE Red-headed Woodpecker, lacked a red head. That's because autumn is the best season to see them here and at that time there are a lot of 'teen-aged' ones whose heads are actually kind of a stripy gray-brown. But they still sport the black back, the white 'tee' pattern from the rear and the snowy white breast and belly.

Red-headed Woodpeckers are robin-sized. This is useful particularly if you can envision a robin clutching the side of a tree trunk. Woodpeckers have a chunky, short-tailed look about them. Their tail feathers are strong, spiked and reinforced in order to serve as a prop to hold the bird against a tree trunk. They actually move around the tree by hitching back on that strong tail and then lunging forward to grab the next spot with their specially designed feet. Their beaks and heads are also tailored to absorb the continuing shock of hammering away on the side of a tree.

Peterson says there are 210 woodpecker species in the world but we only expect six on Nantucket. Not every Nantucket birder gets to see a Red-headed every year.

In a way we are lucky to have them around at all. They were shot frequently at one point in history and Audubon commented on how tasty they were and also felt they should be destroyed as pests since they ate too much orchard fruit and even worse, enjoyed sucking the contents from other bird's eggs!

Arthur Cleveland Bent, whose birding life histories are the source of much of my research, commented that, "The only one I have seen in southeastern Massachusetts, in 50 years of field work, was chased across the line from Rhode Island before I shot it." Perhaps he needed it for his Massachusetts bird list!

At any rate, it is harder to find Red-headed Woodpeckers in New England than in the rest of the country. Historically their numbers have fluctuated wildly, seeming to disappear and then recover strongly. Although the introduced European Starling was once accused of being the cause for the Red-heads decline, now scientists think that habitat loss is the culprit. So many of the things humans like to do – clearcut, develop for agriculture, channel rivers, replace mixed forests with monocultures of pines – all these things make our world seem more orderly but are bad for woodpeckers.

The Audubon Christmas Bird Count (CBC) program provides useful data on population trends for our bird species. CBCs record a 50% decline in Red-headed Woodpeckers since 1966. Our Nantucket CBC shows only a single record, in 1987. Most of these flashy birds move to the southern U.S. for the cold months.

From now until the end of November is the best time to look for them here. Just remember though, you may not see that brilliant red head. Just look for a white on black 'tee' shape as the bird bounds away. That pattern provides the source for an amusing nickname, 'half-a-shirt.' They are a rare find as they return north in May, but if you find one, you'll be seeing as red as you can get!

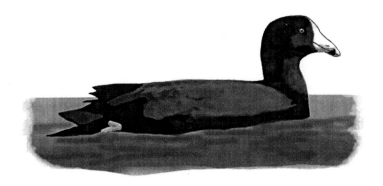

November 11 – Corporal Klinger's Favorite Bird!

If you are a fan of "Mash," you may remember that Corporal Klinger hails from Toledo, Ohio and often speaks lovingly of his Toledo Mud Hens baseball team. Klinger would have been ecstatic in 2005 because the Mud Hens won the International League Governors' Cup.

I always chuckle when I hear that team name because "mud hen" is the nickname for a rather clumsy and humorous bird officially known as the American Coot. I found this creature in my first winter of birding. It was a complete surprise because who talks about coots? I guess they need a better public relations director.

Beginning birders think these are ducks. They are found in the same places, swim in the water and even dive. But if you look in the duck section of your Sibley's guide you'll be puzzled – no coots there. Sibley correctly shows them with the rail family and you have to page through all the hawks and upland game birds before you get to them.

Roger Tory Peterson helpfully includes them with the ducks even though ducks they are not. This is the type of thing that makes his guide so handy when you are learning your birds.

So American Coots are rails, not ducks. Why aren't they ducks? Well one big reason is that they don't have webbed feet, but you can still find them swimming in the water! Their feet have long toes and each toe has a scalloped lobe along it that retracts and extends to make an efficient paddle. These big feet also allow them to walk quite easily in boggy areas and even on lily pads.

Their social behavior is another thing that distinguishes them from ducks. Coots will often cluster together in a tight flock on the water. This is apparently a defense mechanism because when a bird of prey makes a pass at such a group, they immediately go into a splashing frenzy throwing spray into the air and practically disappearing. This continues until the threat passes.

On one occasion when an eagle was the pursuer, an American Coot broke from the flock and tried to run for it, then dove. The eagle hovered overhead each time driving the bird under until it tried to take off and was immediately snatched.

American Coots are about half the length of a mallard, but chunkier. They are the color of dark soot and that translates in Latin to their genus name, *Fulica.* Their conical bills are chalky white in contrast. They also show white under their short tails.

You normally find them in our shallow fresh water ponds fraternizing with the mallards. They often dive for food and then pop up with vegetation draped on both sides of their bill. Sometimes an enterprising mallard will swipe some of this prize.

Taking off is something they do with difficulty. They normally need a long runway and they patter off leaving tracks on the surface behind them. Many times they just crash back into the water, having run where they wanted to go. When they do make it into the air they're an awkward sight, laboring along with their huge feet dangling behind them.

One time I startled eight of them on the North Head of Long Pond. They were in a little pool of open water near the First Bridge and the rest of the pond was ice covered. Off they went but they ran out of water before getting airborne. They slid, rolled and tumbled until they were clear across the ice and into the rushes, never actually attaining flight. What a sight!

After describing their difficulties flying it is amazing to know they've actually crossed the Atlantic and been found in Western Europe on 23 occasions. They apparently migrate at night because you can observe a big flock in a pond but then find the pond empty the next morning.

Coots build a floating nest of rushes and reeds that is anchored to surrounding vegetation so it can't float off. The first of their eggs may actually be laid on this platform before the nest is complete. Sounds almost like a 'shotgun wedding' doesn't it? The clutch may have up to 10 eggs. Coot chicks are not beautiful – big footed, mainly black, with orange hairy feathers on the head and shoulders.

They may nest here regularly but they are so secretive they've only been confirmed once, on Miacomet Pond. If you see American Coots in late May or June, look for those little orange and black fluff balls swimming behind them.

Despite their clumsiness Coots have surprising longevity once they learn the ropes. Banding records show one over 22 years old. I bet that was one that always hung in the middle of that black splashing mass in the middle of the pond.

You can see American Coots here year round. They are rare in summer but very common through the winter unless the ponds freeze solid. Look around the edges of Miacomet, Hummock, and Long Ponds. Quite often one or two will hang around at the duck pond at Consue Spring, particularly when the rest of the ponds freeze up. Enjoy their comical behavior and wonder why anyone would name a baseball team after them!

November 18 – Our Winter Sparrow

No matter how chilly and raw Nantucket is, it seems like a balmy winter resort for many bird species. Myriads of waterfowl sign up to be here every winter but it is the smaller, more fragile birds that often capture our imagination on a frosty morning.

At this time of year a perennial favorite stealthily makes its appearance on the ground under our feeders – the American Tree Sparrow, described perfectly by its Latin name, *Spizella arborea*. They have just finished their summer excursion into the Canadian Arctic where their nest is often lined with ptarmigan feathers. The nest holds an average of five eggs and is never far from the ground because indeed there are no trees over most of their nesting territory.

I have some experience in that climate because Uncle Sam stationed me up above the Arctic Circle in Sondrestrom, Greenland. They told me, "There's a girl behind every tree Kenny!" But of course, the nearest tree was 500 miles away.

The good news for the American Tree Sparrows is that their girls have feathers and they have little requirement for trees. My goodness, why are they called "tree" sparrows anyway?

So many of our birds are named because they reminded early settlers of something from home in Europe. There is a tree sparrow over there that resembles this week's species but it's really not closely related. Now it is known as the Eurasian Tree Sparrow so as not to be confused with our American ones. The introduced House Sparrows that now blanket our country are close cousins.

Anyway that's how our American Tree Sparrows got named. In reality they would be better-named 'brush' sparrows.

This is quite a handsome sparrow with a solid chestnut cap, a two-tone bill, yellow at the bottom, a well defined black 'stick-pin' in the center of its gray breast and two sharp white wingbars on its brown wings. About six inches long they appear the same size as the House Sparrows you see in town.

But these sparrows are not 'townies,' more denizens of the countryside. Driving along the moors near the cranberry bogs you may notice a flurry of them swirl up from the ground into the low bushes. Then if you are patient they will drop back down and resume hopping around feeding. At this time of year, their diet is almost totally weed seeds and they consume prodigious amounts.

Scientists studying them have found over 1000 seeds being processed through a single bird's digestive system. Not long ago when every bird species was evaluated as either harmful or beneficial to mankind, American Tree Sparrows scored high as eliminators of noxious weeds.

So now this species is just making its return to Nantucket having traveled close to a thousand miles from its summer home. A high percentage of them are making the trip for the first time since most of them only live a year or two. But the ones that learn the ropes have a strong homing instinct. Bird banders are always charmed to have one of last year's birds enter a trap to be caught again.

Within a season these are called 'repeats' and it shows how little stress the banding operation places on these feathered mites. If trapped in another year, the term 'return' applies. When the same bird returns to the same spot year after year to be studied, measured and weighed, it feels like an old friend coming back to visit. American Tree Sparrows are known for this type of site fidelity, traveling great distances to drop into the same back yards.

While this seems charming to birders, site fidelity may be disastrous for Nantucket birds. As our island environment dramatically changes, with more huge mansions and landscaped gardens filled with non-native plant species, it can be devastating to these few ounces of feathered vivacity when they return and discover no shelter for the winter and nothing to eat.

Despite all this, the American Tree Sparrow population is still quite high, but mainly concentrated in the central and western part of our continent, where there is less human disruption.

Many who write of winter natural history have been thrilled to the cheerful warble of these hardy little visitors from the North. A. Marguerite Baumgartner, a well-known Oklahoma expert on this species wrote, "I shall never forget my first flock of tree sparrows, feeding companionably at the weedy border of the marsh, hanging on the weed tops like animated Christmas tree ornaments, dropping lightly to the ground and etching their delicate tracery of claw prints in the snow. The air was mellow with their soft warbles, and to me they have always said "Marguerite, Marguerite."

On Nantucket we consider them 'uncommon' from now until the end of April, "present but must be looked for," as 'Birding Nantucket' says. They show up on most of our Christmas Bird Counts with a high count of 51 in 2003. Now and again in April, they will still be vocal and you may hear their charming whistled "Marguerite, Marguerite," as they move through their feeding territories.

November 25 – Yellow Rail

They were a rough-looking crew. They had journeyed from several New England states that winter day, met in Hyannis, and stashed all their gear into an SUV that was then loaded onto the steamer. The crossing had been rough and gray with an icy northwest wind and they were tired and not real chatty as they hit the island. This group of four represented a different breed of birder.

The word had gone out over phone and internet. Yellow Rails found on Nantucket. Just a few days before, a group from Connecticut had been searching a brackish marsh, looking for Sedge Wrens, a rare find. No one had expected Yellow Rails but they saw three!

Now, Yellow Rails are the most secretive members of a whole family that is known for secrecy – rails. More often heard than seen, they are masters of skulking. It's possible to bring them out using recordings of their calls. I've had spectacular experiences with Virginia Rails in a marsh in Colorado where they actually came out and walked around my boots. But without a tape you have to depend on luck. And we don't use tapes much any more since it's viewed as too disruptive.

So what are rails, and yellows ones in particular? Rails are marsh denizens –they like WETLANDS. Seems like humans hate wetlands. They are always draining them. They want to live near them – too near them – sometimes even ON them. On Nantucket the Conservation Commission has the job of protecting them. Anyway, rails live in a vanishing habitat. Coots, which we discussed a few weeks ago, are our most visible rails.

On Nantucket, we find Virginia Rails and Soras (yes, that's their name) in our fresh water marshes, Clapper Rails in salt. Up until the year 2000 we only had a single record for a Yellow Rail and that from 1984 at the end of December. They may be here every year, but it takes huge luck and patience to find one.

How can something hide like this? Well rails just don't typically flush. If they are approached, their tendency is just to freeze or run. Strangely enough, when they run no one notices. I've had them move rapidly around me in the reeds not making a sound or shaking a single stalk. I know they are there because of their calls. It's a strange feeling to have something so close and not be able to see it.

Yellow Rails are the champions at this. They are a little smaller than a starling and are shaped like a baby chicken. Their Latin name, *Coturnicops noveboracensis,* translates to quail-like bird from New York! Ernest Choate, in his "Dictionary of American Bird Names," tells us that second word *noveboracensis,* comes from *novus,* 'new,' and *Eboricum,* the Roman name for the city of York, England. Amaze your New York friends at a party with this one!

They are seldom found in New York. They nest across south central Canada and into North Dakota, Minnesota, and Wisconsin. They winter in the southeastern U.S. and perhaps even Nantucket Island!

They are yellowish brown speckled birds with short yellow beaks, perfectly designed for hiding in marsh grass. In flight, which they seldom use, you see their best field mark – white feathering on the trailing edge of their wings.

Anyway, back to our rail hunters. They came equipped as seasoned hunters would. They were prepared to 'drag' the marsh. A huge hawser was coiled in the back of the SUV, knotted every 10 feet or so for more weight. With knee-length boots and clad like Nanook of the North, out into the marsh we went. Yes, by now I had been enlisted. It was a long rope.

Almost immediately, one of the party went in. A fresh water marsh can be treacherous and he was down above his boot with icy water pouring in. The fun was just beginning. Back and forth across the marsh we trudged for almost an hour. Sedge Wrens we found. Virginia Rails "Wunk-Wunked" at us from the cattails. Alas, I had to leave. Later I learned they managed to flush a single Yellow Rail. The day after this, a horrid northeaster encased this marsh in a glaze of ice that lasted a month. We were convinced the rails left beforehand or froze. Late the following November we went back and flushed two Yellow Rails, birds I'd never thought I'd actually see.

In the 80s you could see a Yellow Rail by journeying in winter to the Anahuac National Wildlife Refuge on the Texas coast. Then you boarded a huge swamp buggy, and were virtually certain you'd see one of these skulkers. But no longer since these huge wheeled vehicles were seriously damaging the marsh habitat. There are no longer any easy ways to see a Yellow Rail.

The good news is they are not rare, although habitat destruction is reducing their numbers both in their summer and winter ranges. No, they are just hard to find. Nantucket birders know several marshes where they might be found from November until things freeze up solid, but most of them are virtually inaccessible to humans.

So, if you see a group of camouflaged people coming off the boat like they are part of a marine landing, maybe they are this year's crop of deer hunters. Or just maybe they are simply pursuing one of the toughest species to add to anyone's 'life' list, a Yellow Rail.

December 2 – The 'Teakettle' Bird

I've heard a lot of bird questions but this is one of my all-time favorites. "I have a bird in my backyard that goes 'twenty-eight – twenty-eight – twenty eight.' What could it be?" Hold that rhythm in your mind. Some people also ask about the 'cheeseburger' bird, or the 'video' bird. I call it the 'teakettle' bird and its official name is the Carolina Wren.

This is a bird I had to go to Martha's Vineyard to see in the mid-50s. Well, I was actually trapped there. Our plane couldn't land at Nantucket. But I had an immense reward because we overnighted with Henry Beetle Hough, Editor of the Vineyard Gazette, and there was a very rare Golden-crowned Sparrow visiting his feeder, a bird that's never made it to Nantucket. So that was a life bird for me, but not the 'teakettle' bird. Later in the day my first 'teakettle' bird wowed me with its trumpeting call from an Edgartown thicket.

I really got to know the bird well when I lived in Atlanta. Being out with the great lister, Terry Moore in 1977, I'd hear a chirp, a whistle, then a growl, then a series of chips, and each time I'd ask, "What's that?" And each time the answer would be the same, "Carolina Wren!" The array of Carolina Wren calls in addition to the 'teakettle' song is amazing.

There are 79 species of wrens worldwide, members of the wonderfully named family *Troglodytidae* – cave dwellers, because of the cave-like nest many of them build. The Carolina Wren is named *Thyrothorus ludovicianus* that translates to "Louisiana reed dweller."

That seem odd, Louisiana – Carolina? Strangely, this species was named by the "Grandfather of Australian Ornithology," John Latham. A medical doctor, he lived in England his entire life, never traveling to Australia. But in the late 1700s collectors from around the world sent him stuffed specimens to be classified and named. Since the first Carolina Wren specimen came from the huge territory of Louisiana, that's how he named it.

Carolina Wrens are the largest wrens in the eastern U.S, but still under six inches from down-curved beak to jaunty tail. They are reddish brown on the back, buff below, with faint barring under the tail. A white stripe over the eye really stands out. Quite often, their loosely attached tail will be cocked in the air. But actually seeing them rather than just hearing them, that's the trick! They are continually moving and hiding. You see a head here, a tail there, almost never the whole bird.

These are relative newcomers to Nantucket, which is right on the northern edge of their range. There was just one on the 1980 Christmas bird count, then none until 1989. Since then they have taken the island by storm with a high count of 157 in 2003.

They arrived on the Vineyard in the 50s. Before that, there had been a remnant population on Naushon Island for many decades. But even in the mid-1900s a warming trend was recognized as species like this one kept expanding to the north.

It's interesting that Carolina wrens do not migrate. They maintain the same territory throughout the year, seldom traveling more than a mile, which makes it more difficult to expand their range.

Expansion actually happens by overcrowding, forcing them to spread out. They probably made it to Muskeget and Tuckernuck before making it to Nantucket.

They are quite adventurous in choosing a nesting site, sometimes in a tree hollow, other times in a thicket. They've even been known to inhabit a sofa that had a hole in the back. The welcoming landlords sat somewhere else for a month while the five young wrens hatched and learned to fly.

Their diet is over 90 percent animal matter, chiefly caterpillars and spiders. So they seldom visit our bird feeders except possibly for suet. I once watched one scramble up inside my gas grill, popping out here and there for five or 10 minutes until he'd caught every spider, all the time "chirrring" to his mate nearby. Quite often a pair of these wrens will sing a duet, one trumpeting the song, while the other one chips and growls in the background.

Since they may not travel a mile in their short lives, it is more likely that they'll stay with a single mate. We know through banding records that one Carolina Wren made it to just under eight years. He was trapped, studied and released 23 times over his charmed life.

Particularly here at the northern edge of their range, our severe climate may shorten their lives. Our wren population 'crashed' early in 2005 when Nantucket was heavily snow-covered for weeks. Evidently these little spider specialists were unable to feed and this was a rather silent spring on Nantucket without their cheery calls.

They are starting to recover now and I'm finally hearing the 'teakettle' bird calling from a nearby thicket. Listen for the spirited song and be amazed that so tiny a bird can make such a racket.

December 9 – Mute Swans -- Not!

In flight they always remind me of the old Concorde SSTs, huge, long necks extended, maybe drooping a little, and stunning pristine white. The scene is the first bridge on the Madaket Road, looking westward. The early sun is shining, highlighting these birds against the dark clouds in the background. Four Mute Swans stroke their way past. There is a haunting sound of wind passing through the pinions of their wing feathers before they coast in for a long gentle landing on the North Head of Long Pond.

These are the swans most everyone knows. I remember the ugly duckling turning out to be a swan. Then there are the wonderful Swan Boats on Boston Common. My Mom took me for a ride there early in life and I remember wondering if these were somehow live swans.

If you see a swan on Nantucket, it is most likely a Mute Swan. These are actually 'alien invaders' from Europe. They were not part of our island bird spectrum as I was learning my birds as a teenager. If you saw a swan here then it would have been a Tundra Swan that is our native swan here in the east.

Whether they were 'planted' here by swan lovers, or whether their range expanded over from the Vineyard, Mute Swans arrived here in the early 60s and have thrived.

Swans have long been favorites amongst humans. Their size, color and graceful actions impress them in people's memories. The Latin name for the Mute Swan is *Cygnus olor,* originating from the Greek name for this species. In Greek mythology swans were associated with Orpheus and Apollo. Julius Caesar reported that the savage tribes inhabiting Britain revered them and wouldn't kill them. Even now, all swans in the British Isles are said to be the property of the Monarch.

In the German opera, Lohengrin, the hero crosses a river in a boat drawn by a swan to defend the innocence of his heroine, Princess Elsa. When Robert Paget built the first of the Boston swan boats back in 1878, he was inspired by this opera.

Then there is the legend that a swan sings a beautiful song just before it dies. Although it is not true, it caused the great Samuel Taylor Coleridge to whimsically write, "Swans sing before they die; 'twere no bad thing/ Did certain persons die before they sing."

So is a Mute Swan mute? Heck no. They make various calls, and the one you are most likely to hear is a threatening hiss. Once when I inadvertently threatened a big cob, as the males are called, instead of running off he turned on me, spread his wings, lowered his neck near the ground and uttered this horrific sound. I backed off quickly. Despite their beautiful appearance, swans are noted for nasty dispositions.

Mute Swans are large, white, with a long neck often 'S' curved. Adults have an orange beak with a black knob at the base. Their legs are black with big black webbed feat. They swim elegantly, long neck raised and usually with the bill pointing downward. They can stand up to four feet tall and are among the heaviest flying birds -- over 20 pounds! Like most larger birds they have good longevity, many living past 15 years in the wild, 35 to 40 years in captivity.

They tip forward to feed, sending the tail up vertically. In this posture they remind me of icebergs floating in the water. Mostly they eat aquatic vegetation and can reach down much lower than the ducks that live around them. But the ducks hang around because frequently a swan drops part of its prize so its neighbors can benefit.

Mute Swans don't migrate like our native waterfowl. When going gets really tough in the wintertime, they withdraw to the salt water. When everything froze solid last winter, Mute Swans became part of the scene off Jackson Point in Madaket where the running tide kept the water open. Many swans succumb during cold conditions like this since they can't feed in very deep water.

There seem to be fewer swans on the island now than in the early 80s. The State Wildlife Service at one time had a program of discouraging these alien invaders by shaking their eggs, disrupting the nesting cycle. Either that or extreme cold has leveled our swan population at around 40 on Nantucket.

They build huge nest platforms in shallow water and lay as many as 10 eggs. It is a five-month period before a young cygnet becomes airborne. Even now this year's crop of youngsters still look a bit brownish.

At this season you can enjoy these avian SSTs at places like Miacomet, Hummock and Long Ponds. You many even find a few cruising the Easy Street basin. If you're really lucky you'll hear the wonderful sound their wings make as they fly past.

December 16 – Another LBJ

Here we have one of the most common winter birds on Nantucket. Yet if you aren't a birder, you probably don't know they exist. Basically another LBJ (Little Brown Job) with some frills, these sparrow-sized birds inhabit most brushy areas on our island from early October until the end of April. They are the eighth most common bird over our 50 years of Christmas Bird Counts, never failing to appear. In 1983 we counted over 5,000 of them.

What I'm talking about here is the Yellow-rumped Warbler, *Dendroica coronata*, the 'crowned' wood warbler. There is a tiny piece of yellow at the top of their heads, at least in spring and summer, but the yellow rump persists all year. A bird's rump is just above the tail, sort of where yours is. So you see the yellow mostly when they are flying away from you.

Until 1973, these were called Myrtle Warblers and most of us birders found that name about right. So-called because when they are here, they feed on the waxy fruit of the myrtle, *Myrica pensylvanica*, commonly called the bayberry on Nantucket. There was a similar species out west called the Audubon's Warbler. It looked the same except it had a yellow throat compared with the Myrtle's white one.

Interestingly enough, these differences appeared during the ice age when the huge glacier came down over the center of our continent and geographically isolated these birds. The ice melted 15,000 years ago and now it's possible for the two races to intermix. Scientists discovered they can successfully interbreed and our Myrtle Warblers and Audubon's Warblers are now Yellow-rumps. The birders rebelled for a while, calling them 'butter butts' but after 30 years we've learned our lesson.

Another reason we fought this move is because, where before we had two species on our life lists, the lists we keep showing every bird seen in our lives, now there was one. If you had just worked very hard to get your four or five hundredth species, you were suddenly one short. About the same time, they lumped two species of orioles together and also four species of junco. Personally I lost five species. I gave up serious bird listing for many years after that.

The good news is the birds don't know the difference. They are just as charming and engaging as always.

As I mentioned above, these are sparrow-sized birds, mainly brown. The yellow rump shows up nicely and with binoculars, you can usually see a yellow wash on either side of their streaked belly. Their call note is a dry "chick" sound and if you learn that one you will be suddenly aware just how many of these LBJs there are around.

These are the hardiest members of the wood warbler family. Warblers are noted for their bright colors and being mainly insect eaters. It's possible to see over 30 different species on Nantucket during the year. In the warm months, Yellow-rumps follow this pattern too. In early April, a marvelous transformation occurs in the males as they go through a molt of their body feathers and become very crisply marked with black and slate blue above, a black mask around the eye, and the four yellow spots, head, flanks, and rump become more dazzling. Birders who have seen them all winter as LBJs now think they are another species!

They nest all the way up to the end of the tree line in the Arctic with just a few breeding as far south as the Berkshires. All summer they feed mostly on insects, sometimes flying quite acrobatically to snap them in mid-air. After raising their four or five young, they molt back into nondescriptness and head back down our way.

In the winter their range is hugely extensive. The great naturalist Alexander Skutch was amazed to note that they were flying around the New Jersey marshes as his ship left New York in December and then a week later in a banana plantation in Guatemala, there were hundreds of Yellow-rumps again, in the open pastures and roadways.

Most Nantucket birders quickly get to love these lively lights of the winter landscape. Since most of them are in their first year, they are supremely curious and respond with vigor to the 'spishing' noises we make to call birds in. Shortly the air is full of their 'chick' call notes and the bushes are jumping with 50 or 60 very excited Yellow-rumps. This is a worthwhile exercise because often they bring in chickadees, kinglets, sparrows, sometimes even a Hermit Thrush with them.

By March we start to hear their wavering whistled song in the air. You'd think that warblers would have a warbling song, but alas most do not. Still, our Yellow-rumps add another vocal dimension to the growing spring chorus of Northern Cardinals, Song Sparrow, Carolina Wrens and American Robins. Most of our 'butter butts' leave before the main warbler migration begins in the spring. Still it is wonderful to have these flashing bits of yellow around for the winter.

December 23 – Horned Grebe

Imagine a bird with a stomach full of feathers – its own feathers! What a shock this is to a beginning bird student when they 'skin' their first Horned Grebe. Yet this is a digestive trick that many fish-eating birds practice. More later – stay tuned!

Have you ever seen a Horned Grebe? If you winter on Nantucket, or summer in North Dakota, you have a good chance. This little duck-like bird has an interesting migration pattern from salt water in the wintertime to fresh water for nesting. It is a cosmopolitan species, known as the 'Slavonian' Grebe in Europe and Asia.

Horned Grebes are small, black above, fading to gray on the flanks and neck with startling white cheeks. The bill is slim, dark and delicate, and if you can see the eye, it is fiery. Back when ornithology involved the use of a shotgun, Arthur Cleveland Bent reported, "I was much impressed with the striking beauty of a handsome male that we *shot*; it had the most beautiful eye that I have ever seen in any bird, brilliant scarlet, finely veined and penciled, with an irregular ring of yellow around the pupil, gleaming like fire in its setting of velvety plumage." It's a shame he had to shoot the bird to gain this appreciation!

"Where are the horns?" you ask. Late in spring they undergo a complete transformation, the neck and flanks becoming chestnut, the cheeks black, and golden shaggy horns stretch back from the eye. We seldom see this striking plumage here since most of them leave by the end of March, but when we do, the birders get excited.

I mentioned they are duck-like. They swim on the water's surface and dive readily. They have the ability to slowly submerge, or swim with just their heads appearing. Holding an injured grebe in hand, early scientists were astonished to see the whole bird inflate as it inhaled, then shrink back down on exhalation. This skill together with the ability to trap air in their roused feathers allows them to act like little submarines.

There are 20 species of grebes worldwide and at this time of year we may see three of them on Nantucket. The Pied-billed is found mainly on our fresh water ponds. The Horned Grebe and the Red-necked Grebe live along ocean beaches. The very similar Eared Grebe has never been recorded on Nantucket, but we watch for them.

The family name, *Podicipedidae*, translates to 'rump footed' in that grebes differ from ducks by having their legs positioned farther astern. This gives them more efficient propulsion under water. Their feet have lobes rather than webs. These are flaps of skin along each toe that flip out to form paddles on the pushing stroke, then cling to the toes on the return.

On land their skeletal design makes it very hard for them to walk upright. Often they push themselves along on their chests. They must have water to get airborne, so a grounded grebe will soon die if it can't get to a liquid runway.

Horned Grebes are regular but uncommon here in winter. This is one of just a few species found on every one of our 50 Christmas Bird Counts with an amazing 214 seen on the 2003 census. On the ocean waves they can be difficult to count because you see them one moment, the next a wave will hide them. When you can see that spot in the water again – no grebe. They have been known to stay under water as long as three minutes, but 45 seconds is more typical. Still, when you are waiting for them to reappear, it can be interminable.

Their nesting territory is mainly north central U.S., across Canada into Alaska. There is a remnant population in the Magdalen Islands in the Gulf of St. Lawrence that is slowly being pushed out by their relatives, Pied-billed Grebes, whose range is being extended further north with global warming.

Horned Grebe nests are floating structures woven into surrounding vegetation. Four or five eggs are laid and when the striped chicks hatch, they jump almost immediately into the water. Often they are seen riding on their parent's backs, nestling into their feathers.

Getting back to eating feathers – even new chicks apparently do this before they have feathers of their own, consuming those of their parent's. Scientists believe that fish eating birds keep a stock of feathers in their gut to prevent their systems from being destroyed by sharp fish bones. The bed of feathers in the stomach slows the digestive process and allows the stomach acid to further dissolve the bones. Studies show over 60 percent of grebe's stomach contents are feathers.

So watch for these horned feather-eaters along Nantucket's beaches through the winter. You'll almost never see them fly. When they finally head off to their nesting grounds, they usually do so at night. Watch for them swimming and diving and with luck you'll catch a glimpse of that fiery eye in your binoculars.

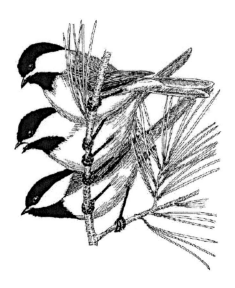

January 6 – Our State Bird

A flurry of wings – a flashing black eye – an electric "chick" sound in the air – the slightest touch of claw on finger – and then gone. A Black-capped Chickadee has just snatched a sunflower seed from my hand and is now jamming it into a crack in a tree in order to break it open and extract the meat.

Here is a bird that even non-birders love. Its personality embodies cheer, spunk, liveliness, and grit. Bradford Torrey wrote in 1889, "It would be a breach of good manners, an inexcusable ingratitude, to write ever so briefly of the New England winter without noting the chickadee … the bird of the merry heart."

Alas, growing up on Chestnut Street in town, this was a bird I could only read about. Chickadees were at best uncommon then on Nantucket, and I had only sparrows where I lived. Our initial Christmas Bird Counts in the 50s only found a few. It was 1976 before the count exceeded 100. Nantucket was a less wooded place then and also fewer people were feeding the birds. Our 2005 count was a record high 616, so chickadees are doing well and Nantucket is a more joyous place because of it.

Chickadees are tiny mites, just a little over five inches from beak to tail. They seem insubstantial, like a good wind could blow them all out to sea. Yet they are fierce in character. When you hold one in your hand for banding it will immediately grab any loose skin it can find and hold on ferociously, glaring at you with its beady little eye as if to say, "You better let me go or I'll have to get rough with you!"

This same spirit shows when they find a predator in their midst. Suddenly there is a frenzy of "chick-a-dee" calls as the flock descends on their enemy, scolding frantically until they draw in crows and jays to finish discouraging the invader.

Surprise – the Black-capped Chickadee actually has a black cap and it says its name – finally a well-named bird. The "chick-a-dee" call is really more of a scolding note. The chickadee's mating song is a whistled "feee-beee" which some people mistake for the Eastern Phoebe's call. But a phoebe actually articulates the word as if spoken, rather than whistled.

Under the black cap chickadees show a sharply contrasting white cheek and then a jet-black bib. Below that they are gray to buff, with darker gray on the wings, back and tail. When you see a chickadee fly across the road in front of you, it doesn't fly so much as flutter. There are little bursts of flapping punctuated by arcs downward. This, coupled with the grayish appearance, makes it seem like a leaf blowing in the wind.

There is much discussion as to whether chickadees migrate. Banding records show that they almost never travel more than a few miles from where they are hatched. Yet in certain years thousands of these birds surge through the countryside in what are known as irruptions. Whether population pressure or lack of food causes this, we don't know. There is still much to learn in our avian world.

What is certain though is that the Black-capped Chickadee population both here and on Martha's Vineyard seldom mixes with other chickadee populations. This geographic isolation is allowing them to become genetically different from other chickadees and they are studied by scientists from Cornell for this reason. Although they look the same, some of our birds have a noticeably different "feee-beee" note that is unrecorded elsewhere. An island can be an interesting scientific laboratory.

Black-capped Chickadees live all across the northern part of our continent, nesting up to the limit of the tree line in northern Canada and into Alaska. Near the Maryland-Virginia line the Carolina Chickadee replaces them. Those look very similar and still say "chick-a-dee" but sound like they had too much caffeine. It is a very fast "chick-a-dee."

Up until the late 90s the Black-capped Chickadee's Latin name was *Parus atricapillus*. But then the birding mavens decided chickadees are very closely related to the titmice that live in Eurasia, so they have been lumped into that genus, *Poecile*. Both are Latin words that mean "titmouse." There are actually seven species of chickadee in North America that are now part of that genus. In Audubon's writings in the early 1800s he referred to this bird as the "Black-capped Titmouse."

Chickadees are hole nesters and will often use a bird box. In lieu of that they industriously excavate a nesting hole from a rotten stump by digging with their beaks. This may end up nine inches deep and then they build a nest in the bottom. Six to eight eggs are laid and four weeks later, the fluffy youngsters are ready to face the outside world. On Nantucket, they nest from May to July.

Although we know these black and white sprites as sunflower seed eaters at our winter feeders, their diet is two thirds insect matter, chiefly the eggs of many species we consider pests.

Last, a quote from Edward Howe Forbush, "The little Black-capped Chickadee is the embodiment of cheerfulness, verve and courage. Follow the call of the Chickadee and it will introduce you to its brethren … a sociable gathering of kinglets, nuthatches, a Downy Woodpecker or two, and possibly a Brown Creeper ..."

So when you watch chickadees, check out the companions traveling with them. Birders know that the key to finding these other shyer and sneakier birds is to first find the chickadee. Listen for their energizing call and let it shine some light on a dull winter day.

January 13 – The Bald Eagle

This is our National Bird, so chosen back in 1782 and oddly one of the first decisions made by our nation's forefathers. It was a controversial one at that. Benjamin Franklin was holding out for the Wild Turkey. Although awesome and inspiring in flight, Franklin felt the Bald Eagle was a bird of bad moral character, eating carrion and stealing fish from Ospreys. But eagles have always captured people's imagination and have found their way onto numerous national seals and crests, so our fledgling country probably felt they couldn't risk choosing a bird that didn't appear fierce.

An eagle's eye view of Nantucket probably starts from over the outer Cape or the Vineyard. High in the air, soaring on long flat wings, Nantucket with its many ponds may seem worth checking out.

Eagles don't make a home here but rather, just vacation like so many others. Most eagle reports are actually Red-tailed Hawks. Few people are prepared for how huge a Red-tailed Hawk can appear at times and they think they have an eagle. When you see a Red-tail in the sky with an eagle, it is like seeing a crow next to a Red-tail. An eagle is almost twice as large as a Red-tail.

Let's get up close and personal with the Bald Eagle, *Haliaeetus leucocephalus*. Actually the Latin name is quite revealing. That first word *Haliaeetus,* goes back to the Greek word for Osprey. Its loose translation is 'sea eagle.' If you do crossword puzzles you know these birds as 'ernes.' There are eight species of sea eagles around the world and this is one of them. *Leucocephalus* means white-headed.

True eagles are in the genus *Aquila*, which is actually the Latin root of our English word 'eagle.' Our Golden Eagles, mainly western birds, are members of this group that feeds much more on rabbits and the like.

Eagles are enormous, with wingspans close to seven feet. An adult Bald Eagle is unmistakable. The body is charcoal brosn and the head, neck, and tail are pure white. The huge beak is yellow. Unfortunately for birders, it takes five years for this plumage to develop. Before that we have mainly a brown bird with increasing amounts of white as the years pass. Most Bald Eagles seen on Nantucket are of the teen-age variety.

To confuse things a bit more we now have Turkey Vultures on Nantucket. These are a bit new on the scene, perhaps due to global warming or just the sloppy habits of some of our deer hunters. These are also huge and are often seen soaring in our skies. But remember, 'vee' for vulture. Vultures tend to hold their wings in a 'vee' when gliding. Eagles usually maintain a flat pattern up there. A friend once described them like a 'flying scarf' with their wing feathers making the ragged ends.

Although this is our National Bird, we have almost killed them off – twice. The first time with guns, the second with pesticide. In Alaska early in the 20th century there was actually a bounty on eagles, as much as $2.00 for a pair of feet. Over 100,000 eagles were killed in this program which was finally terminated in 1953. By then the population had dwindled to 10,000 pairs, but then our use of pesticides and habitat destruction further knocked them down to 500 pairs by the early 60s.

Amazingly, stopping the use of DDT coupled with captive breeding programs has brought this inspiring creature back from the verge of extinction. In Massachusetts there were 19 occupied nesting sites in 2005, 12 of which successfully produced chicks. They are mostly in the Quabbin Reservoir and Connecticut River areas although one nest was as close as Plymouth.

An eagle nest is an amazing structure. The same pairs (they are monogamous) will add to and refurbish a nest year after year until it falls down from its own weight, often in a storm. A nest found in 1713 was over 12 feet high and the contents filled two wagonloads. Strangely, other birds such as Great Horned Owls and House Sparrows sometimes live in some of the 'spare rooms.' Typical nests are over 60 feet in the air in pine trees.

Bald Eagles usually lay two eggs although usually only one chick makes it. It is a long cycle, five weeks to hatching and then another 12 before leaving the nest. Southern Bald Eagles lay their eggs in mid-winter while ours do so in April and May. During the summer, young southern eagles may wander up as far as Canada.

Our records show Bald Eagles appearing on Nantucket in every month except December. Actually our coldest periods are often when they are found. Being fish eaters, they are driven out of habitats where everything is frozen up. Then you may find them around Sesachacha Pond feasting on eels at the edge of the ice. If you see a huge bird soaring that looks like a flying scarf in the air, you may be seeing our National Bird.

January 20 – The Bird in the Sharkskin Suit

That's the way they always appear to me – dressed for business – not too natty – wearing a shiny bluish gray suit with a neat white shirt in front, but no tie.

Herky-jerky they proceed vertically down the trunk of my cherry tree and then flit over for a bite of suet or to dig a peanut from the peanut feeder. I hear their honking call, a bit baser and more strident then the children's party horn of their cousins the Red-breasted Nuthaches.

I think their serious, almost staid, personality adds to the image, something like an old IBM customer engineer who would arrive to fix the printer. "I'm here to do a job, so just let me do it and then I'll go."

Of course we aren't supposed to perceive human characteristics in animals. Scientists point out that animals are animals and humans are humans. But if any of you own pets, I know you'll disagree with this. So let's proceed with this week's bird, the White-breasted Nuthatch, the up-side-down bird.

We have two species of nuthatch on Nantucket, the other – Red-breasted. White-breasteds are larger, six inches from beak to tail. But this is misleading because nuthatches have almost no tails. So that length is mostly body.

Typically you see them hitching their way down a tree trunk; their head kinked back so's to be able to see away from the bark. This nuthatch is blue-gray on the back with a black collar. The males have a black cap atop their head. The females have duller blue. All have white cheeks, throats and bellies – rusty under the tail.

Going downhill, nuthatches gain a different viewpoint of the tiny insects and larvae that hide in tree bark crevices. Other species, like creepers, move upwards along the tree trunk, seeing their own universe of dinner. Between these two groups not much insect life in the bark gets ignored.

The White-breasted Nuthatch's name is *Sitta carolinensis*. *Sitta* comes from the Greek word for nuthatch. Actually, over much of Europe and Asia there is just one species. Saying you have a nuthatch there is quite specific enough. Worldwide there are 31 species and as I mentioned, two of them occur here.

The name 'nuthatch' refers to the fact that when they find food like nuts or sunflower seeds, frequently they carry it off and cache it, bury it in the ground, or perhaps stash it in a tree crevice.

Nuthatches are a cyclical or irruptive group. White and Red-breasted Nuthatches have a three or four year period which you can track quite easily using our Christmas Bird Count data. In 2001, we had just one of each, but in 2005, 38 White-breasted and 161 Red-breasted Nuthatches were found. This doesn't mean the species itself is in trouble, just that they go where the food supply is.

They have good longevity for such small birds, a banding record showing one to have lived almost 10 years. They also have a strong pair bond, so the same couple is often together for many seasons.

White-breasted Nuthatches are hole nesters, frequently using an abandoned woodpecker cavity or a nesting box. They start their nesting in April, lining the bottom of the cavity with strips of bark, then mud, then building an actual nest cup of twigs and grass which is frequently lined with rabbit fur. The five to nine eggs start life in a rather cushy environment. One nest even had most of a whole fluffy rabbit tail within it.

Mrs. Nuthatch does all the egg-sitting but her partner assists by bringing in dinner. This is one species where the parents have to restrain their eager youngsters who often poise themselves ready to launch out into the air but then get driven back inside. I guess it's much like a 14 year-old ready to drive the car.

Family groups stay together into November before turning the children loose to fend for themselves.

Even though the books say these nuthatches are not migratory, they depart our island in the summertime. On Nantucket they arrive in September and are gone by the first of June. A nest has yet to be found on the island. This is a great year to see these little sharkskin suit clad birds. Listen for them honking in the trees around town and then watch for one hitching its way down a tree trunk toward you.

January 27 – Hatched from a Barnacle?

This is Nantucket's other goose, and a bird for which a major Nantucket landmark is named. Brant Point is one of the first things seen as folks arrive here on the boat.

The bird, simply known as the Brant, is a favorite of bird watchers and hunters, but little known by the general public. They don't appear on our ponds and farm fields like the Canada Geese do. Even more confining, they have a real aversion to flying over land. They usually fly low and if they can't see salt water on the other side, they veer left or right and follow the shore.

The Latin name for these beasties is *Branta bernicla, Branta* for the Anglo Saxon word for this species, and *bernicla*, meaning 'barnacle.' Strange folklore from the middle ages caused people to believe that these birds actually hatched from barnacles. As late as 1597 Gerard's "Herbal" stated that, "As it groweth greater, it openeth its shell by degrees till at length it is all come forth and hangeth only by the bill; in short space after, it cometh to full maturity and falleth into the sea." Quite a visual image don't you think?

This is a circumpolar species found all around the northern hemisphere in proper habitat – salt water. But they nest so far north that only recently have nests been found – hence the barnacle story. Most of Nantucket's Brant spend the summer in northern Greenland. Seventy degrees north latitude is the southern edge of their breeding range, well above the Arctic Circle.

How do you know if you are seeing a Brant? Brant are smaller than the Canada Geese we find here, about two thirds their size. They appear black in the front with a lot of white in the rear. Whereas Canadas wear a black stocking over their head with a white chin-strap, Brant have only a faint patch of white on the neck and as Roger Tory Peterson says, "Brant are black to the waterline." They show a fluffy white rear end, the effect accentuated by the fact that they tip forward and send the tail vertical when feeding. You see what looks like a bunch of little white icebergs floating in the water.

So where do you see them? Actually Brant Point is a good spot – not right around the point itself but look across the channel to the eelgrass beds near Coatue. If the tide is right, that's a good spot. An even better one is off Eel Point on Nantucket's west end. Finding a good vantage point can be tricky since you can't get close without four-wheel drive. Looking north from Jackson Point is the best you can do and a spotting scope is required for good looks.

These birds subsist mostly on eelgrass, also famous for being where our beloved bay scallops love to hide. In 1931 a fungus known as the 'eel grass blight' almost wiped out all the eelgrass up and down the east coast of the U.S. This blight almost extirpated these charming birds from our environment. Griscom and Folger in "The Birds of Nantucket" comment they were just starting to return in 1948. They didn't make our Christmas Bird Count until 1977 but have been with us every year since with a high of 614 in 2001. "Birding Nantucket" lists them as 'uncommon' from December through April but you can find them if you know where to go.

We are lucky to have these geese still with us since they have a very unfortunate characteristic – they are really good eating. Arthur Cleveland Bent, whose "Life Histories" are the source of so much of my bird lore commented, "I can not think of any more delicious bird than a fat, young Brant, roasted just right and served hot, with a bottle of good Burgundy. Both the bird and the bottle are now hard to get; alas, the good old days have passed." This was obviously written before Prohibition was repealed late in 1933.

Our area was famous for Brant hunting and until the spring hunt was banned, the region from Monomoy Island to Muskeget was a Mecca for Brant shooters. Box shooting was the style here where they would decoy the birds in and then discharge their guns, dropping many with a single shot, then retrieving them with dogs. On Long Island, 'wing' shooting from batteries was the style and generally deemed more sporting.

So, now through the end of April is a great time to go out and appreciate these rather wild and special geese. Canada Geese are charming but rather too common. The Brant are true survivors of extreme environments and can be appreciated as special members of our unique saltwater environment. Head down to Brant Point at sunset at low tide, and enjoy a really special and unique part of Nantucket's wildlife.

February 3 – To Erupt or Irrupt – That is the Question

"Holy Cow I've found a new bird for Nantucket!" That was my thought back in 1954, with a flock of 150 of these birds around me. My birding bible, Griscom and Folger's "Birds of Nantucket" told me they didn't belong here. It was just my second year of birding and I'm thinking, "No one will believe me."

I was in a grove of pines well out on the Polpis Road. I'd ridden out there on my bike and noticed these birds feeding industriously, taking apart pinecones. Finding they took no notice of me, I was able to walk right up to them. When the cones fell, they would flutter down and continue to work at them on the ground around my feet. Not only were they unexpected, they were also extremely colorful – White-winged Crossbills. It was so perplexing. For a 13-year-old, it was like finding something new to science. How could this be?

It turns out this is an "irruptive" species. Some texts say "eruptive," but, no, these birds don't spew from volcanoes. They are dependent on the cone crop of our northern conifers and if that fails, they "irrupt" in our direction, searching for breakfast. Most of the time, however, their range is far to the north of Nantucket. So why would a bird be so dependent on a single food source? The answer lies in their name - crossbills.

The Latin name *Loxia leucoptera*, means white-winged bird with a curved bill, quite representative after all. But the common name, 'crossbill,' has a rather strange story about it. White-winged Crossbills are known across Europe and Asia as well, where they are known as "Two-barred Crossbills." Legend says that crossbills acquired their crossed bills when attempting to pull out the nails that were holding Christ to the cross. In doing so the birds were spattered with blood, hence their color.

White-winged Crossbills are slightly larger than a sparrow, but chunky. The males are pinkish red with black wings and tail. There are two broad white wingbars on each wing. The females and young are similar patterned but are streaked olive-gray where the males are pink. The bills look heavy and business-like and the upper and lower parts actually cross. This is a special adaptation for extricating the seeds from evergreen cones.

There are two species of crossbills possible here, this one and the Red Crossbill. That species has a similar size and shape but the red is more of a brick shade and there is no white in the wing. It too is an irruptive species but it doesn't always appear the same years as the White-wings.

White-winged Crossbills have a reputation for wandering. They don't necessarily go south in the winter, sometimes heading in the other direction. They've been found up on the Alaskan barrens in the middle of winter where there are no trees at all. When pressed they will eat almost any type of seed or fruit, like juniper berries. They also seem to have a penchant for salt that causes them to fall prey to speeding autos when they go to lick it off the northern highways. Occasionally they get too much salt and become quite ill from salt poisoning.

All this wandering seems to confuse the nesting cycle as well. Something like, "If it's Tuesday this must be Paris!" So crossbills have been found nesting in January and February with deep snow all around. Of course with their food supply high up in a tree, snow is not a problem and perhaps finding themselves in a spot where they nested before in a warmer time of the year, why not?

Since huge flocks of crossbills move together based on food supply, it is unusual to just see one or two. White-winged Crossbills are considered rare here from mid-October until the end of April. But most years there are none and when they do show up you may see a bunch. This is reflected in our Christmas Bird Counts, 34 in 1966 and then almost none until 1997 when 46 were found. Since then we've found some every other year, but never the huge numbers like back in 1954.

With a species that has such a gypsy-like behavior pattern, trying to figure out whether they are in decline is not easy. But scientists have two major tools; Christmas Bird Counts which now track data back over 100 years, and Breeding Bird Surveys that catalog bird populations in the summer months. Between these a downward trend becomes visible.

The National Audubon Society is concerned about many species that depend on our northern forests for their nesting habitat. Between the pressure of logging and foliage damage due to acid rain, this environment is shrinking and White-winged Crossbills are feeling that pinch.

Of course, this is a species that is found all around the northern hemisphere and it is far from endangered. There is even a strange remnant population found in the high mountains of Hispaniola in the Caribbean. For the next few months, watch for flocks of small chunky birds flying into groups of pines. Look for the pink color and white bars on the wings. Then enjoy their trusting nature and bright colors. Remember, they are irrupting, not erupting.

February 10 – My Little Brother the Clown

My little brother is a fascinating and amusing character. Half of each year he dresses in his clown costume and is occupied with thoughts of romance. The other half he sheds his bright colors and heads out to sea, rarely in sight of land.

Now those who know me are saying, "He's an only child." And yes that is true. But 'little brother' is the name given to this bird and his close relatives by the French scientist, Mathurin Jacques Brisson, a colleague of Linnaeus back in the 1700s. The Latin name, *Fratercula arctica*, it translates to 'little brother of the north."

We know this bird as the Atlantic Puffin. Just hearing that name will undoubtedly bring a picture into many of your minds. The puffin's image is on calendars, coffee cups, dish towels, even socks. Heck, my wife is not a birder and proclaims this to be her favorite bird. She is the one with the socks!

The charming poem by Florence Page Jacques starts out,

Oh, there once was a Puffin
Just the shape of a muffin.
And he lived on an island
In the bright blue sea!

Even though puffins aren't much like muffins, many people are taken by them and just enjoy their pictures. The 'little brother' name comes from their resemblance to monk's attire and also because they sometimes hold their feet together as if praying.

Puffins are small, about a foot from beak to tail and are part of the auk family, the penguins of the northern hemisphere. Penguins can fly under water. Puffins fly both under and above the water, although they are much more at ease under water. In the air they flap their wings over 300 times per minute and remind me of giant bumblebees whirring along.

Like penguins, puffins are white on the breast and belly, sharply contrasted with black wings, back and the top of the head. They also have bold white cheek patches. But it is the puffin bill that grabs your attention. It is huge and parrotlike. In the winter it is dark with an orange tip. But come spring the clown costume appears and each puffin grows an orange, blue and yellow patterned mask that covers the bill. They also add snappy vermilion eye-rings and their feet turn from yellow to orange. Boys and girls look alike to us humans.

So much do they look like parrots that they are nicknamed 'sea parrots' and Perroquet Island off the coast of Labrador is the site of one of their larger breeding colonies.

Seldom encountering man, Atlantic Puffins have a trusting and confiding nature that has caused them much grief. Fishermen raided their nesting colonies for eggs and chicks and wiped out the southern part of their range. Gunners found that downing flock members caused the rest of the group to circle and return to aid their injured mates. Even Audubon himself succumbed to the temptation of shooting these engaging targets.

So, by the 20th century most of the puffin rocks off the Maine coast were barren. In the early 1970s biologist Stephen Kress began a program to lure them back, actually using decoys and transporting puffin chicks to imprint them on these historical nesting sites. This project was successful and now puffins nest there spontaneously every year. You can check out Kress's book, "Project Puffin: How We Brought Puffins Back to Egg Rock" from the Atheneum. Nearby Machias Seal Island supports 6,000 puffins each year.

Amazingly it may be global warming as much as hunting that moved the Atlantic Puffins away from the Maine coast. Eskimos in northern Greenland report there are now many puffins breeding way above the Arctic Circle where there were none a few decades ago. So the population has displaced itself northward. Atlantic Puffins are also thought to be among the worlds most common seabirds, with as many 24 million in total.

So with all these Atlantic Puffins we should see them easily on Nantucket – right? Wrong, puffin-breath! Although they nest just a few hundred miles north in the summertime, rather than come south they just go to sea. All six of our Nantucket records are from either dead or dying birds washed up on shore. There are beautiful stuffed specimens that are part of the Maria Mitchell bird collection.

To see my Atlantic Puffins I had to go up to Maine and catch a boat ride out to Machias Seal Island. There we sat in wooden blinds and actually listened to puffin footsteps as they walked along our roof. There were puffins going in and out of the burrows, swimming, diving, and yes even flying around us. It was one of the most magical experiences of my life.

So that is what you must do to see a live Atlantic Puffin. Second best, in the summer go up to the Hinchman House at the corner of Milk and Vestal Streets and perhaps they'll let you see one of these charming little brothers who actually made Nantucket its final resting place.

February 17 – Chattering Silktails

Every time a write an article I find out something unexpected – something new. Waxwings are charming birds that were one of my first surprises as a beginning birder. When someone gives you a bird book, you page through it and certain birds will catch your attention.

The first time you glance at a waxwing, perhaps in your Peterson Guide, you think, "Wow, that's like a little cardinal, except neater." You see the trim yellow band at the end of the tail, the sharply delineated black marks around the eyes and throat, and of course, the rakish crest. The rest of a waxwing presents a gray, Quakerish appearance that blends in with Nantucket. So here you have a bird that is quite a classy dresser without being splashy. Oh, I didn't address the wax on the wing concept. Shucks – wax on the wing – doesn't sound like it would benefit flight much, does it?

The picture shows a striking red patch on each side of the back that is where the secondary wing feathers fold in. This is actually a wax-like tip on the wing feathers that are closest to the body. I've discovered that in the field you seldom get to see this. But the picture shows two different types of waxwings and at first glance you might think the bigger gaudier ones are the males. Actually the big ones are a whole different species of waxwing and are the subject of this week's column – Bohemian Waxwings, *Bombycilla garrulus*.

Here's my learning experience for the week. I discovered that *Bombycilla* translates to 'silk tailed.' It seems that 'Silktail' was the old European name for these birds. But because of the sealing wax-like wing feathers, 'waxwing' became the name of choice. But Bohemian? This is a bit of a mystery. Bohemia refers to a section of central Europe where its thought that the gypsies came from, hence its reference to arty types who disdain conventional behavior.

It turns out that Bohemia is too far south to ever see a waxwing and waxwing behavior is anything but Bohemian. As a matter of fact, Arthur Cleveland Bent's first words about this bird are, "a well-dressed gentleman in feathers, a Beau Brummel among birds."

The other half of their name *garrulus* means 'chatterer.' Again a misnomer. But since they have crests, the namer decided they must be like jays that chatter.

This is the rare waxwing on Nantucket. The Cedar Waxwing is the common one, found here year 'round and even nesting. But Bohemians are almost like the deluxe edition. Instead of just having the little red wax mark on the wing, it is embellished with a white chevron, and then a yellow racing stripe along the edge of the wing.

Obviously they are larger, but that only helps when the two species are together. So the trick is to look at the bellies and under the tail. Cedar bellies fade to a creamy yellow whereas Bohemian's stay soft gray but then have sharply contrasting cinnamon color under their tails.

This species lives all around the northern hemisphere but their summer homes are so difficult to get to that they were little known to science before the 20th century. One scientist commented he had never seen a nest with young in it because the eggs were so rare that whenever a nest was spotted, collectors took it. In North America they nest in far northern Canada from Hudson Bay west to Alaska. Consequently they are much better known from the Rocky Mountains to the west. I remember being charmed by big flocks of them in Colorado Springs.

But like the White-winged Crossbills we discussed a few weeks ago, this is an irruptive species. They are fruit eaters and they really prefer bite-sized berries. I must share with you a mind-boggling list of berries consumed: highbush cranberries, buffaloberries, bearberries, blueberries, wolfberries, snowberries, hackberries, barberries, and the berries of the black alder, American holly, madrona, buckthorn, ivy, asparagus, smilax, kinnikinnick, bittersweet vine, mistletoe, peppertree, dogwood, sumac, laurel, woodbine and the matrimony vine. I never dreamed there were so many kinds of berries!

So if the fruit crop fails where they would normally go, they surge elsewhere. Certain years were recorded as major waxwing years. Literature notes conspicuous flights occurring in the winters of 1908: 09, 1916: 17, 1919: 20, and 1930: 31. You can see there is no specific period for these irruptions but observers actually report flocks in the millions. It is rare to see just one Bohemian Waxwing.

Having said that, on January 1 of this year I was fortunate enough to be out with a team of crack birders the day after our Christmas Bird Count and we did find just a single Bohemian in with a huge flock of robins and the more common Cedar Waxwings. On February 6, 2005, Edie Ray found another single one out in 'Sconset where it was feeding on privet berries.

We've found them on only four of our 50 Christmas Bird Counts. These are rare birds on Nantucket and also very striking to see. So when the word goes out that one is seen, Nantucket's birders scramble. The good news is they are as likely to show up in town as anywhere else. You don't have to stare into an icy gale from Tom Never's to find Bohemian Waxwings. You just need to look into the correct holly tree!

February 24 – Dark, Bizarre Birds from the Italian Theater

What a wonderful day to be atop Sankaty Bluff looking out over the startling blue sweep of the Atlantic towards Pochic Rip. We stand near the end of the ever-shortening walking path with the picturesque red and white striped lighthouse to our left and 'Sconset village to our right, and listen to the rush of the waves and feel the cool air rising from the 45 degree water.

But obviously we are searching for birds and our eyes are attracted to a tightly packed flotilla of ducks steaming along in unison, making you think of a flock of starlings in flight. Suddenly the whole fleet dives, all disappearing in just a second or two, leaving the choppy water vacant. If you were momentarily distracted, looking at a Northern Gannet flying by perhaps, you might feel you had been hallucinating.

But being that high above the water is somewhat disorienting anyway. The ocean seems to have more dimensions from this angle. It's not enough to aim left or right with your scope or binoculars; you must also adjust up and down. So it can be hard to focus on that speck visible to the naked eye. A flock of 20 or so is easier unless the whole flock suddenly disappears.

Today we are discussing a bird that is on every birder's wish list. Looking at your bird book the subtle color combinations jump off the page at you and you stare, mesmerized, thinking, "What on earth is that?" Yet, most non-birders know nothing of them.

This duck is known as the Harlequin Duck, *Histrionicus histrionicus*. Rene Lesson, a French colleague of Linnaeus, named them back in the 1700s. It translates to "a stage player or harlequin," tying to the fact that their colors remind one of the pantomime costumes of early Italian theater.

How to describe this duck? Roger Tory Peterson starts out, "Dark and bizarre," giving us the idea of someone you might meet at a cabaret. The drakes are mainly slate blue with strident white splotches including a dramatic teardrop. The flanks are a handsome shade of brown known as Prout's brown. In sunlight the colors are striking, but so often on this foggy island, the bird you see is dark – and bizarre. The females are dusky with three white patches on their heads, looking more like female scoters.

Griscom and Folger reported this species to be almost unknown in 1948. Indeed I had to journey to Westport, Mass. in 1955 to have one pointed out to me, as it rode up and down in the surf. Thinking of this makes me appreciate the imagery in the Icelandic name for these birds, *brindufa* or 'breaker doves.'

Since then we've learned to locate them here. They've been seen on every Christmas Bird Count since 1985 with a high of 38 in 2000. *Birding Nantucket* shows them as common from mid-December through mid-March.

This is another circumpolar species, wintering along rocky coasts and summering mainly along rushing streams and rapids. Indeed their summer behavior is dramatically different from winter. They are right at home in the most tumultuous rapids, diving and then actually walking along bottom, probing for food. They also chase and catch fish.

They are common in Iceland where they nest on the ground, lining their home with their own plucked breast feathers similar to the down used by eiders. Another nesting place is Ungava at the northeastern edge of Hudson Bay. In Newfoundland and the Maritime Provinces they are common winter residents, known as Lords and Ladies because of the flashy dress of the males.

But it is in the west and Alaska where there are huge numbers of Harlequins. The natives hunt them on Kodiak Island using a unique technique that capitalizes on their diving behavior. The whole flock dives at once and then resurfaces perhaps 20 seconds later. The problem for the ducks is no one is acting as a lookout. When the flock dives, the hunter can approach. When the first one pops up, the hunter hides, advancing only when the birds are underwater. The result is he can approach quite closely and then dispatch a good number with a single shotgun blast. Most sportsmen generally ignore these Lords and Ladies since they are not pleasing to the palate. In Massachusetts hunting of them is banned while we evaluate whether they should be on the endangered species list.

Harlequins have a characteristic known as site fidelity. So both winter and summer, a particular group of birds will return to the same spot. In winter, they favor rocky areas since they are specialized in feeding in that environment. Nantucket has a scarcity of these but for many years, a group would winter next to the west jetty. Now they've moved to area off of Sankaty Bluff where there is a field of submerged boulders.

There are still some spots on the 'Sconset Footpath off Baxter Road where you may catch a glimpse of these Lords and Ladies before they head north in March. The other method is to walk north along the beach from Codfish Park. You should find them before you reach the lighthouse. Late afternoon provides the best light. Otherwise they may appear dark and bizarre.

March 3 – The Bird Under the Glass Dome

There it was inside its tall glass dome atop the bookcase in our sitting room on Chestnut Street. I wasn't allowed to touch it but I was allowed to touch my Grandfather Harry Turner's enormous magnifying glass. I would get up really close to the bird and stare at its white feathers, it's yellow eyes, it's business-like hooked beak.

This week's bird is the Snowy Owl – the owl on the cigar box. Those cigars are still around, even in vanilla and strawberry flavors. So cigar smokers know this bird.

It's a bird people remember seeing. That's because they are special. People see crows, robins, and sparrows and thank goodness, they don't call us every time they do. But when someone sees a Snowy Owl, we hear about it. It's a bird not seen every day. It is 'way cool!'

Its Latin name is *Nyctea scandiaca,* seemingly a strange error made by Carolus Linnaeus, the Swede who pioneered our scientific naming system. *Nyctea* means 'nocturnal' which might appear a great name for an owl, but alas, these are not nocturnal at all. If they were, they would starve. All through the summer this is a bird of the high Arctic. The sun shines 24 hours a day during that period, so waiting for dark would not be a good strategy. Carolus made some mistakes, but he also was one of the most remarkable scientists of his time (the 1700s) and his picture can be found on the 100 Kroner Swedish banknotes.

Snowy Owls are found in Sweden as well as Nantucket. Indeed, they are found in or near the Arctic all around the world, and they are marvelous hunting machines. They are bigger than a crow but appear larger than that, because as most women know, a white outfit can make you look huge. But there's also much size variation in the species. As in most birds of prey, the female is larger than the male.

You'd probably think that all Snowy Owls are white and they are, mostly. Young birds are barred with gray and brown and the big females never attain the almost pure white coloration of the adult males. An older male is stunning, almost pure white with just little flecks of gray on the back and wings. In the wild, the oldest known Snowy is just over 10 years old, but one in captivity made it to 28.

Owls differ from hawks in that they appear neckless. Of course they have excellent functioning necks, it's just like in huge football players, you really can't see them. So the feathering blends the head into the shoulders and also makes it all the more dramatic when the head suddenly swivels around to stare at you, then swivels quickly away and you wonder if you imagined those eyes. Now they're gone.

This illustrates another fascinating owl fact. Like humans, owl's eyes face to the front, not sideways. So like us, they have excellent binocular vision and depth perception. But these eyes are also fixed frontwards, so in order to see left, right, or even behind them, the whole head must whip around. The effect is most entertaining.

Snowy Owls appear on Nantucket in the winter – not every winter but perhaps half of them. They've been found on one third of our Christmas Bird counts with a high of three. That makes it quite amazing that recently four were reported from Coatue, with perhaps another at Eel Point.

Why are they here some years and not others? This is yet another irruptive species and this one isn't dependent on pine nuts. No, it is the life cycle of a small, hamster-like Arctic mammal known as the lemming that controls their appearance here. These furry little critters go through massive population fluctuations, boom or bust. A good year for lemmings is a good year for Snowy Owls and they can stay way up north. If the lemmings would just hibernate, the owls would be down here every year, but that's not what lemmings do. They stay active through the winter so dinner is provided all year.

Periodically, perhaps every five years, there is a massive crash in the lemming population and these wonderful white owls head south. Historically this has been disastrous for them since they are so conspicuous and people shoot them. That's how the one got under glass in our sitting room.

Hunger is a perilous stimulation. In certain years, Snowy Owls head south by the thousands and get shot by the hundreds. In the winter of 1902 nearly a thousand were shot in Ontario alone. Many fly out to sea and land on ships. They've even reached Bermuda, where two were shot in 1843.

The good news is that nowadays they are normally shot with digital cameras and stared at by birders with binoculars. On Nantucket, the places to see them are the beaches at the extents of our island, Great Point, Smith's Point, Eel Point, and Coatue. Normally by the end of March they head north, seeking a spot where the sun will shine 24 hours a day and they can scrape a depression on the ground and lay their seven or eight eggs and feast on lemming. If you miss them this spring, look for them on the beach next December.

March 10 – The Many-throated Mimic

This marvelous bird was named for its wonderful singing ability and so-named by a man who never got to hear it. This was back in the 1700s when the idea of recording a bird song and playing it back was so fantastic no one could conceive of it. Mark Catesby was an English naturalist who lived in the Carolinas in the 1730s. He gave this bird the common name of 'Mock Bird of Carolina' and his written description of its song inspired the Swede, Carolus Linneaus, to create the Latin name *Mimus polyglotos*, 'many-throated mimic' for this week's bird, the Northern Mockingbird.

When I was learning my birds in the 50s it was just the Mockingbird. I found it somewhat ironic that later on the birding gurus added the word 'Northern' to the name, particularly since it is the state bird of five states in the southeastern U.S. Down south, the bird is ubiquitous, hard to ignore. But who would want to? They are such a charming part of the landscape.

In Harper Lee's *To Kill a Mockingbird* the bird becomes a metaphor for the well-mannered, relaxed, genteel style of southern life. The woeful target of little boy's air rifles, the message being it was sacrilege to kill one.

Here on Nantucket it is described as common year 'round although we may be stretching that over the past few years. In our relatively northern climes we are near the edge of this awesome bird's range. When a cold snowy winter like the one of 2004-5 hits us, these birds take quite a blow. Like cardinals, mockingbirds stay in the same place all year. It was population pressure or perhaps global warming that brought them to us. Other factors include the clearing of the land, lawns and gardens. Mockingbirds are well adapted to living around human habitation.

In many ways though this gray clad, Quakerish-looking bird is a wonderful match for Nantucket's somber color schemes. Mockingbirds have a body about the size of a robin, but with a much longer tail. They are part of a New World family known as mimic thrushes that also includes catbirds and thrashers. They are gray above, lighter gray below, with flashy white wing and tail patches. These really only show in flight and are quite visible as the bird flies away from you, swooping up to perch. When the wing is folded the white patch shrinks to two wingbars.

But it's probably their voices rather than their appearance that make you aware of these polyglots. If there is a mocker nearby their vocality makes them hard to ignore. In the winter, they maintain a feeding territory and announce this with an utterance I call the 'scissors snip.' Imagine a large pair of pinking shears munching their way through a bolt of cloth.

But in March, the real fun begins. The longer days trigger the annual nesting cycle and Nantucket's Northern Mockingbirds are bursting into song. The trick is knowing what you are hearing. Yes, they do mock other bird's songs and that can be confusing. You may hear the song of a Carolina Wren, Cardinal, Killdeer, or the screaming of a jay. I've been fooled many times by the skill of a mockingbird. The tactic is to home in on the source and see if the song changes. Other birds repeat the same song over and over, but mockers repeat each phrase four to six times, and then move on to another.

Another bird that is a fantastic mimic is the Lyrebird of Victoria, Australia. In the Dandenongs, I would hear a Whipbird, then a Bell Mynah, then the sound of a motor drive for a camera, all coming from the same thicket.

Many people ask, "Why do some birds do this? What benefit do they gain from copying another's song?" Perhaps it's just another way of claiming a territory. It makes it sound like the place is already spoken for. Indeed, when people kept mockingbirds as caged birds in Europe, their singing had an intimidating effect on the native birds around them. Even the nightingales became silent.

Which draws us to another subject – nighttime singing. Northern Mockingbirds are famous for singing on moonlight nights. People tell of a mocker sitting atop a chimney and the song literally filling the inside of a house as it radiated out through the openings in the fireplaces.

In the deep south, Northern Mockingbirds may raise three broods a year, so the songs go on from May through October. It's an awesome experience to see a singer atop a phone pole, singing passionately, and then launching himself up in a somersault to emphasize a particular phrase.

Hopefully over the next few years our 'Mock Bird' population will recover. I miss hearing them in Monomoy like I used to. But out near Bartlett Farm there is still an active group. Listen for them when you visit that area and imagine Spanish moss and magnolia trees.

We'll have to talk about Northern Mockingbirds more in a future column. With that many voices, there is a lot to say.

March 17 – A Very Famous Duck

You are probably thinking, "Daffy!" or perhaps "Donald!" But no – this one is famous as a game bird, and it is the true epicure who knows it.

Birders know it as the Canvasback, in Latin, *Aythya valisineria,* a celery eating water bird. This is a one reason for its good flavor. Over much of its winter territory wild celery is its favorite food. So instead of tasting fishy like many of the diving ducks, this one is a 'sweety.'

Many of you may not know a Canvasback from a 'greenback' so here is what we are talking about. They are slightly larger than a mallard but there the comparison ends. I've never seen a Canvasback at Consue Pond or in someone's front yard. They are diving ducks and really not at home in such places.

Canvasbacks have lovely white to grayish backs that have a canvas like appearance, chestnut red heads over black breasts and black at the tip of the tail. But their main distinguishing feature is their Neanderthal-sloping foreheads. Their beaks are long and seem to slope directly to the top of their heads. Mrs. Canvasback has the same shape but all the colors are washed out.

I looked up the definition of 'canvas,' wondering about the color, and discovered that the original cloth product was made from hemp. The word canvas actually comes from the Arab word for 'cannabis.' One always wonders where artists get their inspirations.

But back to the celery! In the early 1900s this bird, along with the stewed terrapin of Maryland kitchens, caused Baltimore to be known as the gastronomic capital of our country. This is because Chesapeake Bay is a winter magnet for Canvasbacks and this is where they feast on *Vallisneria spiralis*, the wild celery. You'll note the similarity with the Canvasback's name above. Our wild celery was named in honor of an eminent physician and naturalist, Antonio Vallisneri, from the 17th century. Recognizing this, a bad-spelling ornithologist passed the name on to the Canvasback.

Anyway, it is the wild celery that makes Canvasbacks such good eating. Fattened on the roots and buds of that plant, this duck may weigh in at six pounds. Around here there is little wild celery so instead they feast on fish, mussels, and other aquatic animals. This is difficult work, so our Canvasbacks are tough and fishy, not a good 'table' duck. Audubon noted this himself in years when the celery crop was bad.

Nantucket hosts these handsome ducks (actually Arthur Cleveland Bent calls them 'lordly') from October through April and they are common during the middle of that period. They have been counted on every Christmas Bird Count since 1965 with a high of 605 in 1976.

Originally they nested in the prairie pothole habitat of the Dakotas but as that habitat was turned into farm fields, Canvasbacks were driven farther north. This human interference has put pressure on the population and two U.S. States have them on a 'watch' list. You are still able to hunt them in Massachusetts.

Canvasbacks lay seven to nine eggs in their down-lined nests found along the reedy edges of Canadian marshes. Quite often there will be a few Redhead or Ruddy Duck eggs in the nest as well. Apparently if you really need to lay an egg, any nearby nest will do. The hens do all the incubation and rearing of the young. The drakes head off to party as soon as the eggs are laid. Canvasbacks are not poster children for women's liberation.

A favorite method of hunting Canvasbacks involves 'tolling' whereby a small dog is encouraged to run up and down the beach retrieving balls or sticks, quite often with a red or white handkerchief tied to its collar. Curiosity brings the ducks in close enough to shoot and then the dog is used to retrieve them. This is how the Nova Scotia Duck Tolling Retriever got its name.

As is often the case with waterfowl we know a lot about movement and longevity due to the return of bands placed on them.

Some canny Canvasbacks have survived a long time, over 22 years in the wild.

Good places to find Canvasbacks on Nantucket are the North Head of Long Pond, Hummock Pond near the ocean beach, and in Sesachacha Pond. You might confuse them with the Redhead that has a similar colored head, but they lack the lovely white back and that sloping forehead. They are out of season now so don't even think about whether they are tasty!

March 24 – "Swampy"

A swamp, bog, bayou, marsh, mire, quagmire, morass, or slough – could this be home sweet home? Actually the Free Dictionary on-line adds the further distinction, "A seasonally flooded bottomland with more woody plants than a marsh and better drainage than a bog." Now we are getting somewhere, we can scratch off a bog as too wet and a marsh as not wooded enough.

What's in a name anyway? This bird was originally known as the "reed sparrow," a name given it by the eminent early American naturalist, William Bartram. Bartram published "Travels through North and South Carolina, Georgia, East and West Florida, the Cherokee Country, etc." in 1791, considered to be one of the foremost books on American natural history. Bartram went on to spark Alexander Wilson's interest in birds. Wilson later inspired Audubon, so you see an interesting chain of events.

Audubon and Wilson have many species named for them. Bartram was only memorialized with the Bartramian Sandpiper, an interesting mouthful, now simply known as the Upland Sandpiper.

His "reed sparrow" was given the translated Latin name "the Georgia song finch" in 1790 by the Englishman John Latham (also known as the Grandfather of Australian ornithology). It seems that scientists all over the world would send John specimens and since this one came from Georgia, and looked like a Song Sparrow, it became *Melospiza georgiana.*

Bartram's student, Alexander Wilson, gave this bird its common name "Swamp Sparrow" in 1811, and that name has stuck. My dear friend and mentor, Edith Folger Andrews, simply calls it "Swampy," when it shows up at her feeding station.

This is another 'little brown job' or LBJ as birders refer to them. As such, non-birders lump them into the mass of mouse-like creatures that are hardly worthy of mention. But put binoculars on them and you begin to appreciate their charm.

Swamp Sparrows are slightly smaller and more trim than the ubiquitous House Sparrows you see around town. They have a chestnut cap, gray-trimmed face, and are mainly gray to buff underneath with a fairly sharply defined white throat. The wings can appear quite rufous and have no wingbars. The lack of a wingbar is an important way to make sure you are not seeing a Field or American Tree Sparrow.

Alas this is a species you are not likely to see unless you are in or very near one of those swampy habitats mentioned above. Birders know where and how to find them. One of the first clues is the sound they make. During most of the winter we only hear the contact note. This is an, "I'm here. Where are you?" mechanism that most species use. It is a high-pitched metallic 'clink.' Your first thought on hearing it would be "White-throated Sparrow," but the second clue is where the call comes from. If it is a fresh-water marsh, think, "Swamp Sparrow."

Getting to see your quarry is the next exercise. Avoid trying to approach the bird. They are much too smart for us. Their response to a threat is to drop down under the bushes and run like the wind. But like our feline friends, their curiosity is their undoing. Try making a 'spisshhhing' sound, repeated over and over, a favorite birder's trick. This quite often causes Swampy to pop to the very top of a bush where you can admire it. Keep calling and you may be rewarded with a close view. Then you can tick off the field marks and see how different these marsh-dwellers actually are.

This species is actually quite abundant over eastern North America. They nest from the Mason-Dixon Line north through much of Canada, even as close as the Cape. In winter we are on the northern edge of their range which extends all the way down into Mexico. Our Christmas Bird Counts have picked up this species on almost every count since 1964 with an amazing 48 spotted on our most recent one.

On Nantucket we only find them in the cooler months, arriving in mid-October and staying until early June. April and May are excellent times to spot them because migrating birds swell the winter population. Also this is when they actually start to sing.

The song is a rapid high trill on one pitch reminding birders of a Chipping Sparrow or even a junco. The key again is where you hear it coming from. Swampy never gets far from his wet roots.

Good places to find them on our island include the Lily Pond, the marshy edges around Long and Hummock Ponds, and along the marshy trails at the Grace Grossman Environmental Center on the Polpis Road. Try "spisshhhing" into the swamp and see what pops up.

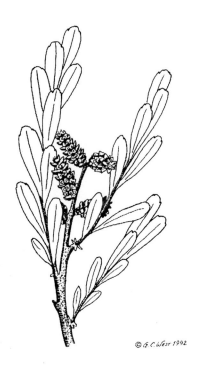

© G. C. West 1992

March 31 – Re-'mock'- able

Two weeks ago we launched into a discussion of *Mimus polyglottos*, our very own Northern Mockingbird, talking about how they live here year round but are near the northern limits of their range.

Actually, global warming or not, mockers have been island residents since the early 1900s, but like the Carolina Wren, winter can be tough on them. In 1995, our Christmas Bird Count found 98, on the 2005 count, only one. The preceding winter was a tough one and Mother Nature can be a harsh taskmistress.

The Sunday birdwatchers were recently treated to a pair of these long-tailed birds near the millpond on New Lane. In case you've forgotten, mockingbirds are robin-sized but stretched out, gray above and below with a white splotch on the wing and snappy white flags on either side of the tail. The brushy-edged habitat of the millpond is an example of habitat they like. Eileen McGrath reminded me of another. There is a theory that the mockingbird's spread to the north has been helped by the plantings along the median strips on our Interstate Highways. Good or bad, one of the highway designer's favorite offerings is the Multiflora Rose, itself an alien invader from Japan. So as our Interstate Highways spread north, *Rosa multiflora* spread with them, providing a habitat and food supply for the our mockingbirds. Certainly the steady increase of the mockingbird population here through the 60s, 70s and 80s would appear to support that.

Like true islanders, mockingbirds stay here year 'round. The same birds are with us winter and summer. Since they can't take advantage of the Stop and Shop, their diets must change. Winter mockers live on our berry crop, holly, privet, poison ivy, and rose hips. During the summer they become more interested in insects. It's not unusual to see mockers hopping along a lawn rather like robins.

This lawn hopping demonstrates two other interesting habits. Often you will see a mocker make a little run along the grass, then stop and arch its wings upward, exposing the white wing patches. I've even seen the fledglings do this with wings scarcely able to sustain flight. A few steps – stretch, a few more – stretch, even standing on tiptoe to do this. Scientists are still guessing at the reason for this behavior, whether it may startle an insect into showing itself or perhaps just shading an area for a better view. Seeing a group performing this ritual is quite amusing.

Another lawn behavior features two mockers, their breast feathers inflated to make them look larger, hopping back and forth facing each other along an imaginary line across the grass. Some think this is a courting display. I am of the school that says this is a territorial dispute between two males defining exactly where the border between their two territories will fall.

In the earlier column I mentioned the symbology within the novel, "To Kill a Mockingbird." This week let me add the Mayan legend about the mockingbird family that was so poor they could only dress in dingy attire. The rich chief's daughter was a cardinal who aspired to be a great songstress. While the cardinal took lessons, the mocker hid in the bushes and practiced too. Finally the day came for the cardinal to prove herself, and, realizing she still had no singing voice, she begged the mockingbird to help her. Hiding in a woodpecker hole, the mockingbird sang while the cardinal lip-synched (perhaps beak-synched) and everyone applauded, except the rich chief who saw through this ruse. He brought out the mockingbird and proclaimed it the greatest singer of all. Since then the mockingbird has always outsung the cardinal.

Mockingbirds are also famous for the spirited way in which they defend their territory. I've had people perplexedly tell me about being 'attacked' by a bird while just walking across their yard. Most any dog or cat owner has heard a tale of a pet being driven away from a mockingbird nest, occasionally with the bird actually riding on the pet's back.

Of course this gray bird's main claim to fame is its wonderful singing. People keep records of how they do it. One comment, "Thirty-two different birds mimicked within 10 minutes." C. L. Whittle in 1922 told of a bird imitating 39 bird songs, 50 birdcalls, plus a frog and a cricket.

Each time you hear a different song, the phrase is repeated four to six times, then on to another. Over a 10 minute period one mocker changed songs 137 times. You definitely get the feeling they are just showing off. Frequently they will be perched at the top of a tree or pole, and sometimes actually turning somersaults in the air as they strut their stuff.

With luck over the next few months, you will be living near enough to these "Re-mock-able" birds that you'll get to share in this wonderful show. On Nantucket, listen for them doing the Northern Cardinal, Carolina Wren, and the Killdeer.

April 7 – Battleship Ducks

That's what the big drakes always make me think of –
battleships. They're long and low in the water and, at least on Nantucket,
there aren't very many of them. You see big flocks of other ducks but
these are few and far between.

In Europe they're known as 'goosanders.' Here they are
mergansers – 'diving geese.' Three species of these 'diving geese' grace
our waters, the Red-breasted –common in salt water, the flashy Hooded –
seen in the cricks, and this one – now known as the Common Merganser.

When I began birding back in the 50s, we called them American
Mergansers, a separate species from the goosanders across the ocean.
Now the birding mavens have found them all to be the same species,
Mergus merganser. They nest throughout northern U.S. and Canada, and
all the way across Siberia into Scandinavia.

Mergansers are actually very interesting ducks. Some fables start
out, "Long, long ago when chickens had teeth...." Well it seems like this
family of ducks actually has teeth! Merganser beaks are long and narrow
with a bit of a hook at the end. Along the side are saw-like serrations
which help them hold onto the fish they catch. These beaks are certainly
nothing like Donald Duck's bill.

Common Mergansers are large, bigger than a mallard, and their long white waterline emphasizes this. Female Common 'Mergs' look much like their Red-breasted Merganser cousins. They have a rusty head with a shaggy crest behind, often looking like they're having a bad hair day. The back is gray and they are white below. Whereas the Red-breasted's neck fades from rust to white, Common Merganser females have a sharp dividing line.

The drakes are radically different. Their heads are bottle green and round, showing no crest at all. The brilliant white from the neck down and back along the flanks contrasts sharply with the dark colors above. The saw-toothed bill on both sexes is bright red as are the feet. In flight, the drake's black and white wing pattern is quite striking.

Their nesting habits seem odd for ducks. Typically they use an old woodpecker hole perhaps 40 feet up in a tree. You'll see a duck perched on a limb nearby, or fly directly into the tree and disappear.

When it is time for the 10 or so chicks to vacate the nest they often drop from the nest and either bounce on the ground or splash into the water. Occasionally Mom merganser is seen to carry them in her beak.

By the way, Dad gets no points in this liberated society. Drake mergansers feel their job is done as soon as the eggs are laid. But don't be too hard on them because, like many waterfowl, this is the time they are flightless.

Most ducks go through a cycle known as the 'eclipse.' They actually molt all their flight feathers at the same time. A complete body molt accompanies this and, for a time, even the brightest drakes look like their drab lady friends and most are grounded. The hen mergansers go through the same process later than the drakes. Because of the eclipse it can be very hard to find many duck species in August and September.

Mother merganser and her chicks can be quite engaging to watch. The ducklings swim and dive quite early in life and are extremely buoyant, reminding you of a string of bathtub toys following their Mom. They may even ride on her back.

I mentioned that mergansers are fish eaters and from this you can infer that they are diving ducks. They actually hunt in packs, driving fish into the shallows and then pursuing them relentlessly. Sometimes they swallow a fish that is too large and the tail protrudes from their mouth until the head is digested. Their digestive chemistry must be amazing.

You can find Common Mergansers on our island from December through the winter months and then tapering off in April. During the early 20th century they were almost unknown here, but they've been found on every Christmas Bird Count since 1975 with 50 of them in 1995.

On Nantucket, the best place to find Common Mergansers is the North Head of Long Pond. Go to the First Bridge and look between the two Osprey poles. Good binoculars are a requirement and a spotting scope is even better since they seem to favor the far shore. Go there early in the day when the light is behind you and see if you can find a duck battleship!

April 14 – The Perils of the Purple Finches

If you feed the birds you are probably thinking, "I have these guys in my back yard." You may be right. But there are finches that are purple and there are Purple Finches. Chances are the purple finches you have in your back yard are actually House Finches, *Carpodacus mexicanus*. The charmers we're talking about this week are close cousins, *Carpodacus purpureus*, a different shade of purple, and the plot thickens.

Back in the mid-1800s before we started tampering with our environmental mix in the eastern U.S., the Purple Finch was a very common summer resident in southern New England. All that changed when we introduced the House Sparrow from Europe. These aggressive and very fertile guests pushed out a number of native species. In 1906, William Brewster lamented, "Since the English (House) Sparrows became numerous the Purple Finches have abandoned one favorite urban haunt after another, and, excepting at their seasons of migration, I seldom see or hear them now in the older settled parts of Cambridge."

And this was just the first chapter of the perils man has brought on these oh-so-gentle and pleasant avian citizens. More on that later. In the meantime, just what is a Purple Finch?

Roger Tory Peterson's description starts out, "Like a sparrow dipped in raspberry juice." That puts an image in your mind. He also uses an amusing adjective to describe the bill, "largish." Actually all finches have fairly substantial bills, capable of cracking seeds. But Roger is helping us separate Purple Finches from House Finches, which is a bit of a challenge for beginning birders.

The unfortunate fact is you are likely to see many more House Finches and, as Mr. Brewster pointed out, few Purples. And now it's time for chapter two of 'The Perils of the Purple.'

When Brewster was concerned about the shortage of Purple Finches, their only problem was competition with the new House Sparrows. In the 1940s and 50s, pet stores in the eastern U.S. started selling House Finches. This was actually a western species (hence the Latin name referring to Mexico), not found here. They called them "Hollywood Finches." Back then, there was no restriction on keeping wild birds in cages. When the law was passed making it illegal to do this, the pet stores opened their cages and House Finches were released all along the east coast.

The results of such actions are always more complicated than anyone would imagine. But apparently there was a niche here in the east for House Finches and they turn out to be very successful competitors.

Nantucket Christmas Bird Count data starts in 1955. We can see Purple Finches appearing on about half of the counts, with a high of 38 in 1970. The House Finch arrived in 1975 and quickly became common year 'round. Every year we count hundreds of them but seldom more than 10 Purples. So, most of the year if you see a finch that is purple, chances are you are seeing a House Finch.

The good news is that from now until mid May you also have a good chance of experiencing a real Purple Finch. One of your first clues may come through your ears. Purple Finches make sort of a flute-like tooting noise when flying. This is their 'contact' note. Contact notes have an "I'm here. Where are you?" type of function. Their actual song I'll describe by relating it to the House Finch's song.

You hear House Finches singing frantically now almost all over the island. It is a rapid series of whistled notes, typically ending with an upward trill. It has an exciting sound, but not really a lovely one. When you hear a Purple Finch is makes you think of a House Finch that has had voice training. The melody is smoother, mellower, and slightly less hurried, almost like a torch singer compared to a rapper.

If you are lucky enough to see the singer it will most likely be a male, although the females sing a bit as well. The plumage is more pink compared to the reddish look of a House Finch. Also, the males have no streaking underneath.

Mr. and Mrs. Purple Finch look quite different, something scientists refer to as sexual dimorphism. Mrs. Finch has missed out on the raspberry juice. She is brown, stripy but brown. If you notice an eye stripe and what looks like a moustache, you have a female Purple. Mrs. House Finch has a very bland face.

Bird banders tell these two species apart as much by behavior as appearance. Strangely enough, the more laid back Purple Finch turns out to be a biter. They are given the nickname "Furple PINCH" because of that. House Finches are very docile in the hand. The other characteristic is that when they are released, the House Finch calls but the Purple flies away silently.

So if you have House Finches coming to your feeders, watch over the next weeks for these Purple cousins. They'll stay with us until mid-May before journeying up into Northern New England to nest high up in spruce trees. They'll be back in September if they survive the perils of the summer.

April 21 – A Crossword Puzzle Bird

Sacred bird of Egypt – four letters. That's the family of our bird this week. Actually this bird's relatives also include spoonbills, herons and storks. Oh – and if you guessed "ibis," you are right on track.

We have one ibis that occurs regularly but rarely on Nantucket – the Glossy Ibis, *Plegadis falcinellus*. In fact the name is redundant, both words meaning "sickle-billed," although one word comes from Greek, the other Latin. The word "ibis" goes back to ancient Egypt where there is a species known as the Sacred Ibis. The Egyptian moon god Thoth is represented by an ibis in hieroglyphs because of the similarity of the curved ibis bill to the new moon. At one point in Egyptian history millions of dead ibis were mummified and buried, honoring Thoth.

Glossy Ibises are fairly large, measuring longer than a crow, but much of that is beak and legs. They look dark until you catch them in sunlight, then stunning green, bronze, and mahogany sheens dazzle your eye. The other striking item is the very long, down-curved bill that it uses to probe deep in the marshes for worms and crustaceans. The first time you see one you might think you have found a black curlew, a common nickname for this species. But a curlew is a sandpiper and not a close relative.

Ibises like to nest in bushy river marshes, typically three to 10 feet above the water. They quickly build a nest of sticks just before egg laying starts then keep adding to the nest throughout the season. Three or four eggs are laid but incubation doesn't start until laying is complete. So all the chicks tend to hatch at the same time. Observation shows both parents sharing incubation, one bird sitting for hours at a time before being relieved.

The meeting and greeting ceremonies are quite unusual in that there seems to be a large amount of physical affection between mated pairs. Observers write how this display goes on for about 15 minutes with much bill rubbing, cooing, and mutual preening of each other's feathers, reminding one of honeymooners. Other species of ibis aren't nearly so affectionate.

When Griscom and Folger penned the original "Birding Nantucket" back in the late 40s there was only a single record for this species, that being one that was shot in September of 1869. In reality, this was when Glossy Ibises were first appearing on our continent.

Like the more recent arrival, the Cattle Egret, Glossies are a Eurasian species that has found its way across the Atlantic from West Africa to Brazil and then spread north. In the early 20th century it only nested in Florida but they are strong fliers and go on exploratory missions after the breeding season. But unlike the Cattle Egret, this species specializes in marshes close to salt water, so that limits its range.

Nantucket's second recorded Glossy Ibis was an exhausted bird found at Codfish Park in April of 1958. Elmore Davis found the bird and Edith and Clint Andrews went out and collected it. She still remembers the bird standing on a stool in their kitchen. The species was almost unheard of here so what an exciting moment that was. Unfortunately the bird was too traumatized to survive. It is now part of the Maria Mitchell Association bird collection.

In Massachusetts, Glossy Ibises were first found nesting in 1974 and there was a quick surge that brought the population up to 170 pairs in 1976. Either due to habitat loss or other factors known only to the birds, this level was not sustainable. We now have around 20 pairs along the Massachusetts coast from Duxbury up towards Newburyport.

Most of the time it is extreme weather that brings them to Nantucket. We consider them rare but regular from the beginning of April through mid-November. They have never nested here.

When you see them here, it's most often in flight. You see a few dark birds with long beaks and long trailing legs flying rapidly in formation. With the call, "Glossy Ibis," birders frantically grab for their binoculars, because many on Nantucket have never seen one.

A few years ago, one spent several weeks flying back and forth between the millpond on New Lane and the Lily Pond. Last year one spent a week or 10 days prowling the edge of the cricks not far from the Rotary. The word flashed like a wildfire around Nantucket's birding community and soon spotting scopes and cameras were taking advantage of this avian treat.

Other places to search are the salt marshes near the University of Massachusetts Field Station and also out on Eel Point. If you find one of these 'black curlews,' study that long down-curving beak and think of the new moon and how so many of these birds were made into mummies honoring the moon god back in Egypt.

April 28 – Pining Away?

One hundred years ago this was a really rare bird on Nantucket. Why? No habitat! Sure the island was still here but throughout the 19th and early 20th century it was virtually treeless. The forest that was here when the European immigrants arrived got in the way of their sheep raising plans on the island. It was also cut to build houses and of course was the principle source of heating fuel.

In the early 1840s our whaling prosperity had caused the population to grow to over 10,000. When the famous naturalist Henry David Thoreau visited here in 1854 he wrote in bemusement, "There is not a tree to be seen, except such as are set out about houses."

Because of the Great Fire of 1846, the Gold Rush, and demise of the whaling industry, by 1880 less than a third of the population remained. The last sheep departed in the 1940s and Nantucket is now being reforested.

But this is a bird column and you are probably wondering when we'll get to that. Our bird this week is a warbler. Warblers in general are hard for non-birders to get to know since they don't come to bird feeders; they're small, and easy to miss. But it's an amazing family to study. Actually 37 species may reach Nantucket every year and six nest here including the one in this column. The warbler family includes some of the most colorful and spectacular of American birds.

This species was actually given two different names by early ornithologists. Their appearance varies so much it's easy to get confused. Bird books can only do so much. My friend Granger Frost says, "People all look different. Why shouldn't we expect the birds to do the same?" This warbler may appear almost gray and then go through various levels of brilliance to the extreme where the breast and throat are bright greenish yellow blending to an olive-green on the head and back. Two white wingbars mark the wing and there are white spots on the outer edges of the tail. What controls this is age and sex. Adult males are the brightest and first winter females, the dullest.

We're talking about the Pine Warbler, *Dendroica pinus,* literally the dweller of the pine trees. Its favorite habitat is Pitch Pine forests that are quite common on Nantucket. But this brings us back to the beginning because these forests are a fairly recent development here. They grow quickly in our sandy soil so they are the first vestige of the island's reforestation process. The Pine Warblers love it now, but in future years, more and more of the pines will be replaced by hardwoods.

Pine Warblers are hardy. Considering most warblers subsist mainly on insects, winter on Nantucket doesn't work for them. But these birds switch over to seeds and fruit and are also very good at finding insect larva high in the pine needles. So with even a few degrees above frost, they can get some animal protein.

Not found on our Christmas Bird Counts until 1981, they've been almost constant with a high of 24 birds in 2004. They hang around through most winters but you have to work hard to find them. This is not so by the time we reach mid-April. Then the increasing solar cycle causes them to start thinking of mating and dramatic territorial behavior starts. The first evidence of this is song. The Pine Warbler is one of the few in this family to actually 'warble.' When you walk near even a small grove of pines you may hear it. Their song is a high-pitched trill often varying slightly in pitch.

If you feed the birds anywhere near pine woods suddenly, in mid-April, Pine Warblers will find you. Suet feeders bring them in but they are also partial to peanuts and even seem to eat sunflower seeds, quite amazing with their puny little warbler bills. Right now there is a riot of green and yellow around my feeders, often they are even hopping on the ground, picking up what has dropped from the feeders above. They don't seem to understand how dangerous we humans are and will land only a few feet away and sing – quite a dramatic performance.

Pine Warblers usually nest from 10 to 30 feet up in a pine on a horizontal limb. The nest is well-concealed in pine needles and, as is so often with bird nests, the construction is fascinating. They are early nesters and feathers are frequently used to provide a warm lining. One nest on the mainland was completely lined with bluebird feathers – quite a sight! Four eggs are usually laid and the nesting season runs from May through the end of July. The show doesn't end then since Pine Warblers continue singing into September.

Great places to hear many Pine Warblers in concert include the State Forest between the 'Sconset and Polpis Roads along that little stretch of the bicycle path, and also in the other section of the State Forest that is off of Lover's Lane.

If you hear the song, see if you can locate the singer high in the pines. Often if you use the birder's "shpisssshing" noise, they will come right down for a closer look at you. The time is right for Pine Warblers here on Nantucket now. With fewer pitch pines in the future, your children may be missing them.

May 5 – Birding the Wave

Imagine a huge wave rushing across the Atlantic toward Nantucket at over a thousand miles per hour. Actually you don't have to imagine because this event happens every day. The wave of which we speak is the gradual increase of light called dawn.

Dawn is the period from when you can barely discern the first light in the eastern sky to when the sun finally breaks the horizon. Nantucket's nesting birds ride this wave from beginning to end for they sense first light long before you and I can.

It's spring and some birds are so full of passion they sing off and on all night, particularly with a full moon. Mockingbirds and cardinals are famous for this and in Europe – the Nightingale.

But the big stars of our dawn are the American Robins. At this time of year they start caroling around 3:30 a.m., two hours before actual sunrise.

The noted ornithologist, Arthur Cleveland Bent wrote, "The robin is apparently the first New England bird to awake in the morning. A few males begin to sing in darkness, at the earliest dim sign of approaching dawn; soon, as the light strengthens, more and more birds awake and join the singing until, gaining in volume, the song swells into a general chorus which lasts all through the morning twilight."

The peak of the robin wave here is between four and five a.m. Wonderful if you love their "cheer-up-cheerily" but perhaps bad if you are having a hard time sleeping.

Quoting Bent again – "William Brewster was much impressed by the element of drama in the great wave of robins' song which sweeps overhead every morning during the breeding season in the darkness before daylight, and continues on, westward, keeping pace with the sun, but beginning far in advance of its light, as it moves across the continent from the Atlantic to the Pacific."

Years ago my first experience of this wave was several thousand miles west in Colorado Springs. Riding through town towards my work at the Air Force Academy in my little MG convertible, the continuous chorus of robins overhead seemed like heaven to me. Nothing else was stirring. They owned this section of longitude as the dawn flew past.

Robins even start calling before the roosters do. On Nantucket it seems there are more roosters around these days and they don't sound off until just after 4 a.m. Just about the time the first Song Sparrows begin their 'hip-hip-hooray-boys – spring is here!' song. Shortly after that, the Gray Catbirds start their squawking cacophony. Our summer catbirds have only just dropped from the sky in their return from their winter homes in Florida, so their part of the chorus is not well established yet.

At about 4:30 a.m. you can barely make out the faintest glow in the eastern sky. The Northern Cardinals come fully alert and immediately start their daily territorial assertions. They do this by singing stridently at each other; their songs often begin with a whistled, "What-Cheeeeer!" In years past I would hear the first 'cough' of a Ring-necked Pheasant, but alas, all the development and feral cats in Monomoy have driven them away.

By quarter of five there is a pink glow on the eastern horizon and shortly thereafter you may hear the first 'coo' of a Mourning Dove. Just after five the Carolina Wrens begin their boisterous three-syllable "weed-eater" song. The robins have been going for more than an hour and are just starting to taper off. The birding wave is moving west.

A few moments later the first whistled 'fee-bee' notes of our chickadees cut the air. This is their 'love song' and when we first hear them giving it in February, it's a nice sign that spring is on the way. The "drink your teeeee" call of the Eastern Towhee begins and now the robins have fallen silent, perhaps thinking about donuts at the Downyflake.

As the sun breaks the horizon the chickadee 'fee-bee' notes are almost continuous. It's as if the second stanza of the chorus has begun. Often at this time there will be an explosion of crow calls. When crows find a roosting hawk or owl, they go into 'mobbing' behavior to try and drive this individual away.

Between sunrise and six o'clock the last members of the choral group rouse and start to contribute. The jumble of the House Finch and the ecstatic exultation of the American Goldfinch ring through the air.

A week earlier and we would have had the 'Old Sam Peabody' of the White-throated Sparrows. They've been practicing their renditions since late winter but now most of them are in northern New England, doing it for real.

If you have to be up early these spring days, step outside and listen, particularly between 4 and 5 a.m. You'll hear the marvelous chorus of robins all around you and you can just imagine the slope of the big wave of daylight sweeping westward toward us.

May 12 – Our Very Own Willy Wagtail

The Willy Wagtail is a favorite bird of the Australian Bush. It's a small bird, a flycatcher and is always wagging its tail as its name implies. Our bird this week is also a tail wagger and a favorite because it often nests around human habitation and ingrains itself into people's consciousness.

Most non-birders don't know about flycatchers. They sound like a great thing to have around. Actually, as a youngster, I thought they'd work out well in the outfield for the Redsox, but that's another story. Flycatchers as a group make their living by sailing out from an exposed perch to take an insect on the wing. This type of move makes them very observable and also gives birders a great show.

This week's bird is the Eastern Phoebe, Latin-named *Sayornis phoebe*. There are actually three species of Phoebes but the other two, the Say's and the Black, live in the west. The Genus name *Sayornis* translates to "Say's Bird," and therein lies a great story.

Thomas Say was an entomologist – that is – he studied insects. He accompanied Major Long on his 1819-20 Rocky Mountain expedition. He was a prodigiously active scientist who discovered many new species of both birds and insects. He also mentored Charles Lucien Bonaparte (Napoleon's nephew) who went on to be one of the principal natural scientists of the mid-1800s. Sadly Thomas Say died quite young and when Bonaparte made the decision to split the three phoebes off into their own Genus, he named them for Mr. Say. A western phoebe is named for him three times with a Latin name of *Sayornis saya,* plus the common name, Say's Phoebe.

Phoebes all say their name, a name that goes back to Greek mythology, it being the name of one of the 12 Titans. When I tell you it 'says' its name, it actually utters the syllables in a buzzy way. The call is a contact note as well as a territorial warning. If you are near an excited Eastern Phoebe, you will hear "Phoebe" 30 times a minute. It's not an overpowering sound but it insinuates itself into your consciousness.

Phoebes are small, just a bit larger than a sparrow, and sit very erectly on their perches. The tail wag is diagnostic, slowly lowered and then snapped back up, really more of a twitch. This is very useful because phoebes appear a bit nondescript, dark gray above, contrasting with whitish below, no wingbars or eye rings.

Being flycatchers you don't expect them to be around here all year and we start looking for them by mid-March. A few of them nest here in the summer. Back in the 50s there was a bridge under the Polpis Road that hosted a pair for many years. They love to find a ledge that is sheltered from the elements upon which to stick their nest, carefully crafted from mud, grass fibers, hair, with an outside layer of moss for camouflage.

This often places them in close proximity to man, particularly in rural settings, and they are seen as sociable companions through the warm months, subtly repeating their call and also ridding the neighborhood of many noxious insects.

They are often quite creative in their choice of nesting sites including around a light socket, partially supported by the wire; on a hook inside an old well or on a strip of wallpaper dislodged near the ceiling. Many times the nests are placed in such a way that the young birds' first trip away from the nest must involve flight through tortuous obstacles to get to a safe perch.

In 1840 John James Audubon was fascinated by the Eastern Phoebes that lived near him in Pennsylvania. Bird banders acknowledge him for being the first to place a primitive band on one of these in order to determine if they would return to the same spot the following year. Quoting Audubon, "When they were about to leave the nest, I fixed a light silver thread to the leg of each, loose enough not to hurt the part, but so fastened that no exertions of theirs could remove it." He was excited to note that one of his phoebes returned to nest the following year.

These charming flycatchers sometimes hang with us long enough to be counted on our Christmas Bird Counts, having been found on eight. This reflects their hardiness as many Nantucket winters don't set in until January, and also their ability to switch over to small berries when flying insects are scarce.

This year if you journey to the parking lot at Windswept Bog off the Polpis Road you may hear an Eastern Phoebe constantly telling you his name. Perhaps he is a descendant of the phoebes that used to live nearby 50 years ago.

Can you think of other birds that say their names? I'll mention a few of them for you at the beginning of next week's column.

May 19 – Cross-dressing Sea Snipes

Well, this week's bird does NOT say its name, but last week I promised you a few who do. How about the chickadee and the towhee? Can you come up with another one?

This week's bird doesn't say much at all. It's not a songbird. Actually it is one of those birds that tantalize us in our bird books but we almost never see. Mariners would see them well out in the ocean and nick-named them 'sea snipes' because they reminded them of that marshy denizen. Their real names are phalaropes. This is a strange family of birds – perhaps one of nature's experiments.

As a high school student back in the 50s I read "Too Late the Phalarope" by Alan Paton, thinking it was going to be about birds. It turned out to be a social commentary on life in South Africa, but it still brought me the feeling of these interesting birds whose sexual roles are reversed.

Phalaropes are sandpipers that swim. Good thing too, since they spend a huge amount of their lives far at sea. The one we're homing in on this week is the Red-necked Phalarope. It used to be called the Northern Phalarope before it was lumped in with other phalaropes that live across Europe and Asia. Their Latin name *Phalaropus lobatus* means 'coot footed.' Coots (see "Corporal Klinger's Favorite Bird!" in an earlier column) have lobes on their toes that act as little paddles when they swim.

This is the time of year to see Red-necked Phalaropes on Nantucket, but first you must have really rotten weather. When we have the easterly storms that cause the wind to howl and the rain to fly, then these pelagic seafarers get blown in to land. You may remember that in May 2005 we had a very cold northeaster. First phalaropes showed up in Miacomet Pond near the barrier beach and later they were in the pond at Great Point.

Recently another storm brought phalaropes in all along the east end from Tom Never's around to Hoick's Hollow. These were mostly Red Phalaropes, a close cousin, but that same storm brought many pelagics close to shore all along the Massachusetts coast.

How would you know a phalarope? They are very similar in appearance to the clockwork toy Sanderlings we see on so many of our ocean beaches. The difference is they are stretched out fore and aft so they have a delicate streamlined appearance and you never see them scampering in the wash of the surf. No, you find them out in the water swimming, usually in tight circles.

Much is written about their graceful fairy-like appearance. They don't actually dive into the water. They are so buoyant they can hardly submerge to bathe. Their circling causes tiny sea critters to rise to the surface where they can be plucked.

The most striking characteristic is the way the sexes differ. Some birds are very sexually dimorphic and almost always it is the males who have the bright colors and the females that are drab. Phalaropes are the opposite. The ladies wear the gaudy plumage and the males are relatively nondescript.

The roles are also reversed through the courtship cycle in that the females do the displaying, enticing the relatively disinterested males to mate. The males construct the nests and after the females lay their four eggs, the males do most of the incubating and chick rearing and the girls head out to party for the summer.

Red-necked Phalaropes are small, no more than eight inches from beak to tail. They show a stripe on the wing in flight, mainly gray above and white below. Females show a striking rufous red patch across the throat and up behind the ear – also gold bands across their back. The bill is black and needle-like.

Although rarely seen, they are not rare birds. There are thousands of them passing by us now, 10 or more miles off shore, headed up to northern Quebec and Ellesmere Island. Other Red-necked Phalaropes fly across the Great Plains to the western part of the Canadian

Arctic. Their wintering grounds are in the Pacific off Central and South America. These tiny birds have a tortuous journey to make every year and, as difficult as their life is, it's not surprising that the oldest one on record had survived just five years.

Maybe we'll be lucky and have no more bad easterlies this spring, but if they come, ride out into the teeth of the gale and stare out into the waves. Afterwards check our ponds near their beach barriers. They may also show up in October under similar circumstances. You are in for a colorful treat.

May 26 – "Just a Little on the Trashy Side"

I'm not really into Country & Western music but I enjoy a tune by a band called "Confederate Railroad" that goes "Too much lipstick, too much rouge, Gets me excited, leaves me feeling confused."

When I started researching this week's bird it made me think of this tune, for its Latin name *Pheucticus ludovicianus,* translates to "painted with cosmetics from Louisiana." My friend Pete Sawyer called me recently excited about having seen one. "The most striking bird I ever saw," he said. Profound words from an octogenarian.

When Baron Karl Ludwig Freiherr von Reichenbach named this Genus in 1850 he was obviously impressed with the lovely rose color which seems rouge-like. This same splash of color caused my Dad to be sure one had bled to death after crashing into his window. It was only after closer examination that he realized it was just shockingly red feathers contrasting with the white underparts.

We're talking about the Rose-breasted Grosbeak, a very charming bird, and a joy to have in your neighborhood. I remember that when I was a lad our house was a-buzz because one had been seen in our japonica bush in our side yard on Chestnut Street. Perhaps it was my grandmother's excitement about seeing it that first sparked my interest.

The common name 'grosbeak' comes from French for a huge beak and it certainly is one of the major characteristics of this species. Actually our Northern Cardinals were at one time called "Cardinal Grosbeaks" for their similarly large bills. These bills handle sunflower seeds with ease.

One's first thought in seeing an adult male Rose-breasted Grosbeak is a big, chunky, black and white bird. Then he turns towards you and your eyes get knocked out and your socks roll up and down your legs! What a beauty! This bird sports a bright crimson cravat below a black throat and a pure white breast. The gross beak is white and there's a glitzy black and white pattern above. In flight there is a stunning series of black and white flashes from the wings. The rose also shows under the wings.

Mrs. Grosbeak is an entirely different story. She is speckled and striped with brown and white, no black, no rose. She looks like a big sparrow. Where the males show rose under the wings, she shows yellow. However both sexes show the same demeanor. They just seem to radiate dignity and contentment.

When they arrive on our island at the end of April and early May they descend on our bird feeders as if they'd never left. Perhaps you have houseguests like this. They walk into your living room and plop themselves down in your favorite chair and look so comfortable you're glad to have them there.

The other joy they bring us is with their song. Most of you know the 'cheer-up – cheerily' of the robin and it's always nice to compare a song to that if you can. Rose-breasted Grosbeaks sound like robins with a WD40 injection. The whistle is more liquid, slightly quicker, and often with an actual 'wolf whistle' included. If you don't hear the song quite often the call note will key you to them. If you remember the wood on wood squeak you used to hear from an old gate latch, that's what it sounds like.

Unfortunately these charmers don't nest here. They will hang around singing their lovely song into early June and you think, "Maybe this is the year they'll do it." But then they disappear. Nantucket's woodland habitat just isn't quite right.

Where they do nest it is not hard to find them. The nest is not high and the male does quite a bit of the incubation himself, even singing while on the nest. One of my most charming experiences was looking down from the road going up Mount Greylock in western Massachusetts and seeing a male on the nest softly singing that lovely liquid warble to himself.

Second year males are often flecked with brown amidst the black and don't attain full plumage until age three. The oldest wild Rose-breasted Grosbeak lived almost 13 years. They used to be a popular cage bird when it wasn't illegal to keep them and one male made it all the way to age 25. The owner of a 15-year-old bird reported that at that age all the white parts had turned a rosy red – what a sight to see!

When they arrive back here in late August and September we get many duller hatch-year birds. They are on their first journey into the tropics where they charm the folks who live in Guatemala and points south. Their wonderful song however, is reserved for the springtime and Nantucket birders always feel lucky to have heard it.

June 2 – New Bird in Town?

The bird world is always changing. People ask me, "Are there as many birds as there used to be?" They're worried that we're damaging the environment and making the world into a place where birds can not survive. Of course we are, but the good news is it will take us a long time.

The short answer to the question is, YES! The longer answer leads us into this column.

This week's bird is not a bird of the Americas – at least not originally. These birds blew straight across from Africa into northern South America. The first sighting was in Suriname in 1880. From there they have spread across our whole hemisphere. The first recorded U.S. nesting was in Florida in 1953. Now they've been found in all 50 states reaching Alaska under their own power and having been introduced into Hawaii in 1959. This is an amazing avian phenomenon.

We're talking about a small white heron known as the Cattle Egret, *Bubulcus ibis*, and the only member of its genus. The Latin translates to – an ibis that likes cattle. It is certainly found around cattle but an ibis it is NOT! Its contentment around cows tells us why it has become so common and also why it seldom occurs here.

Cattle Egrets are crow-sized in length but a lot of that is long legs and neck. It is the only small white egret with a yellow beak. Another common name it goes by is 'Buff-backed Heron' because in the breeding season the top of its head and back pick up that color.

These herons depend on water less than any of their relatives. They prefer pastures and farmlands because their diet is mainly insects. You've probably seen pictures of them perched on the backs of cattle where they wait to catch a grasshopper stirred up by the animal's grazing action. Here they hang out with cattle but where they come from they are seen on wild buffalo, rhino, elephant, hippo, zebra, giraffe, eland, and waterbuck. They are known as cooperative feeders since they are not competing with their traveling companions for food.

Humans with their predilection for raising cattle have provided just the habitat these white birds are looking for. Our first one was at Eat Fire Springs out on the Wauwinet Road in April of 1960. Yes, they had cattle out there then.

We have one or two Cattle Egrets show up on Nantucket almost every year. But we consider them special and when they are found, island birders scramble to see them. This year one was seen in early May out on Hummock Pond Road. There are some lovely brown cows grazing out there and somehow this bird found them. But more often they show up in a meadow where cows might graze, if we had more of them. They've been found along the Polpis and Madaket Roads and even around the Mill Pond on New Lane.

The fact that they show up here illustrates the behavior that has allowed them to spread. They are just natural wanderers, perhaps explorers rather like us humans. When not actually nesting, they just disperse in all directions, seeing the sights!

They nest in colonies with other herons, building their stick nest in low trees and laying three to five light blue eggs. The mating process is a bit odd in that when the males do their displays, posturing with their buff colored plumes, the females will actually jump on their backs to claim them. After these details are worked out, both partners work together to construct the nest, the male bringing in sticks and the female weaving them together. Both parents incubate and share in the upbringing of the chicks. A Cattle Egret may live as long as 10 years.

These birds are very social and gather in flocks of hundreds where they can find food. Often they follow a tractor that is plowing.

They are also attracted by brush fires, feeding along the edges, catching little beasties that are fleeing from the conflagration. Airports are another haunt – not right on the runways, but along the edges where they wait for the wash of aircraft to blow insects out of the grass.

Cattle Egrets now outnumber all the other egret species in America. Our native species were badly persecuted by plume hunters at the beginning of the last century and their numbers were down just when these aggressive new interlopers were arriving.

So are there as many birds as ever? Yes, but they are different birds. Man has transformed this planet and made it just fine for some species, but uninhabitable for others. Cattle Egrets have found what we do just right for them and have spread and multiplied in response. But our gentrified island will never collect more than a few. Island birders have to scramble to see them or go elsewhere.

June 9 – Marathon Bird

My mother always used to tell me it was bad manners to talk with my mouth full. Yet this week's bird almost never shuts up. Hour after hour they call, 60 to 80 times a minute, one phrase piling atop the last.

This bird is a vireo, a word coming from the Latin *viridis* meaning green. But its pedigree goes back earlier than that since Aristotle himself referred to vireos being entirely green and easily caught. Aristotle's vireos were actually European Greenfinches. In the Americas vireos are a whole new family of birds that also bear the Genus name, *Vireo*.

There are nine species that occur in the eastern U.S. and Roger Tory Peterson suggests we break them into two groups – those with wingbars and those without. This particular vireo falls in the wingbar-less category and has the common name, Red-eyed Vireo. Like so many common names, it may lead new birders astray, searching for a red flash in the eyes. In fact, the red eye is hard to see and is only present in adult birds. The full Latin name is a bit more useful, *Vireo olivaceous,* olive green.

Vireos are sparrow-sized birds and used to be placed next to the huge wood warbler family in your bird book. Bird books follow a complex process called 'taxonomic sequence' which is a major hurdle for new birders to get past. Basically, birds in your field guide are placed in the order of their evolution. American bird guides generally start with loons and end with finches – water birds to land birds. Newer bird guides throw us yet another curve, moving ducks, geese and swans to the first position.

Ornithologists still argue about such things and in the new "Sibley Guide to Birds" vireos are much earlier, between flycatchers and jays. They are grouped with shrikes. Shrikes, also known as 'butcher birds,' are songbirds that eat other songbirds and small rodents, impaling their prey on hawthorns to make it easier to rip them apart. Vireos share the shrike's nasty hook at the end of their bill but stick to insects rather than attacking their feathered kin. In South America there is a family known as "shrike vireos" which sounds really cool.

So, our Red-eyed Vireos are quite green looking when seen from above, whitish when seen from below. They have a black bordered eye stripe and a bluish gray cap. On Nantucket we look for them from early May through October, but looking is not the way to find these birds, rather, you should be listening.

The Sunday bird watchers experienced this recently out on Almanack Pond Road. The song was in the background, subtle but incessant. To me it's like a slow-motion robin song. Each phrase is spaced out, rather than running together in the robin's "cheerup - cheerily."

Naturalist Wilson Flagg commented in 1890 "We might suppose him to be repeating moderately, with a pause between each sentence, 'You see it. You know it. Do you hear me? Do you believe it?' All these strains are delivered with a rising inflection at the close, and with a pause, as if waiting for an answer."

This is a rare song to hear on Nantucket, but in mainland forests Red-eyes are part of a continuous, day-long concert. A student at the College of Forestry in Syracuse once quizzed me, "What bird is known as the 'great marathoner'?" Since I was living in an area where I heard them all the time, 'Red-eyed Vireo' was an easy answer.

If you read my column 'Birding the Wave' a few weeks ago we talked about the 'dawn chorus,' a daily crescendo of bird song. But these 'great marathoners' continue on all day, subtly adding phrase on phrase of music for us. In the heat of mid-day, the Red-eye sings alone.

Red-eyed Vireos build their hanging nests seldom more than 10 feet high in the hardwood forests at the east end of our island. They raise their four young and then start their journey south late in August. But once migration begins these marathoners fall silent. Those we see here in September and October hardly utter a sound except for a querulous snarl when alarmed.

Neotropical migrants, they travel huge distances each year, nesting as far north as the Canadian Maritimes and then travelling south as far as Brazil, mainly taking the land route through Central America and Panama.

If you go into Masquetuck or perhaps walk the wonderful trail in Squam Swamp be sure and listen for the measured phrases of this great avian marathoner.

June 16 – Roseate Terns

Have you noticed the birds on the Massachusetts Endangered Species License Plate? You have to look closely and perhaps use some imagination. They are those two little squiggles just above the flukes of the Right Whale – Roseate Terns.

What the heck are they? This is a wonderful family that makes you think of silver swallows over the sea. I last wrote about terns more than a year ago. Roger Tory Peterson tells us there are 44 species worldwide. "Birding Nantucket" shows 11 species usually occurring on Nantucket every year.

Terns, aside from being a favorite crossword puzzle seabird, are close relatives of gulls. But compared to gulls, they are like ballerinas to long distance runners. Their wings are longer, thinner, and more pointed. Their tails are generally forked, sometimes with long streamers. Their flight is more buoyant and graceful, but with none of the long glides and sweeps that gulls perform.

They range in size from the tiny Least Tern, under 10 inches, to the Caspian Tern, Herring Gull size. In between are the "MST"s as birders call "medium-sized terns." The two most likely found here are the Common and Roseate.

It was those long tail streamers that caused terns to be almost driven to extinction by plume hunters around the beginning of the 20th century. It was not unusual to see a lady's hat with a whole stuffed tern atop it. With legal protection these birds slowly recovered their numbers but Roseates have lagged due to their habitat restrictions.

Roseates are the most maritime of the terns, almost never leaving the salt air behind. In reality they spend most of the year at sea, only visiting the edges of land when it is time to raise their young. Historically the largest colony in the northeast was found on Muskeget Island, between Tuckernuck and Martha's Vineyard.

This tern's Latin name honors the Scottish scientist who first recognized it as different after he shot one on the Firth of Clyde in 1812. It is *Sterna dougalli,* for Dr. Patrick MacDougall. This also gives us a clue that this tern's range encompasses both sides of the Atlantic. *Sterna* itself is the historic Latin word for tern.

We used to identify terns by bill color – Arctic with blood red, Common orange with a black tip, and Roseate solid black. Life was simpler then. Now we know that bill color varies with season and age and we seek out subtler differences. Your main task on Nantucket is to distinguish Roseates from the more common, Common Terns.

The Roseate is known as the most ethereal member of this graceful family. Their long tails extend well beyond their wings when resting. Their usually black bills are longer, thinner and more pointed. In flight their wings seem silvery white all the way to the tip compared to the dusky black of the Common Tern's. This works very well except in the autumn when another MST, the Forster's, makes its appearance with white in the outer wings sharply contrasting with gray over the rest of the back.

Like many terns, Roseates are long-distance fliers, following both sides of the Atlantic to winter well below the equator. They completely leave the U.S. in winter. Audubon noted the first Roseate Terns as they arrived in the Florida Keys on April 10, 1840.

Their close relative, the Arctic Tern, holds the long distance migration record with an annual round trip of 22,000 miles. That averages more than 60 miles a day – every day!

On Nantucket, Roseates arrive at the west end of the island early in May, about the same time as the Common Terns. At that time it's possible to actually view the pinkish tinge on their upper breast for which they are named.

Where Roseates nest they are always in close proximity to Common Terns. Indeed many Common Tern nests have Roseate Tern eggs in them and vice versa. Their two or three eggs take three weeks to hatch and the fuzzy sand-colored young are quickly mobile and even swim readily. This is their time of greatest vulnerability and both Herring and Great Black-backed Gulls feast on a lot of them.

When the chicks are out you often see adult terns flying along carrying fish, usually Sand Launces, to feed them. They poke the whole fish headfirst into the chick's gape and let their throat muscles finish the job. Often the fish is too long for the digestive system and you see chicks placidly sitting with a protruding fish tail.

Roseate Terns are on both the U.S. and Massachusetts Endangered Species Lists. They exist in several fragmented populations around the world, each one at risk to man's omnipresent shoreline development. Other persecution is less subtle. In the Maria Mitchell bird collection, there is a specimen that was found dead from a bullet wound in 1983.

The best places to see Roseate Terns are the bars at the end of Eel and Smith's Points. We are still hoping to find them returning to their old nesting grounds out on Muskeget. You may find these graceful birds around our island until mid-October.

June 23 – Some Call Them Quail

    Here is a bird most Americans can identify by call alone. A few weeks ago we talked about another that says its name – the Killdeer. This week's bird not only speaks his name, but you may know people with that name – Bob White. The official name is the Northern Bobwhite. Hunters often simply refer to them as 'quail.' The Latin name is interesting in that the genus, *Colinus* comes from the Central American Indian name for a partridge, *zolin*.

    Back in the 50s when I was learning my birds, this was a common bird on Nantucket. I would hear the whistled 'Bob – White' call everywhere in the woods along the Old South Road. I would search and search for the singer, whistling the call back to him, and hardly ever saw one. The call is ventriloquial. Somehow I would always look in the wrong direction and the singer, motionless, remained a mystery.

This is a bird that is on the edge of its range on our island. So much so that it has to be restocked regularly by sportsmen to maintain its presence. Although there were many in the 50s, Griscom and Folger in "The Birds of Nantucket" (1948) comment that "The last Bobwhite on the island flushed on Joy St., July 10, 1942." Whoever it is that does this restocking doesn't report it, so it's always a surprise when we start hearing the clear whistled "Bob – White" after a few years' absence.

This bird is much beloved by the general public. First there is the ubiquitous call, second their rather engaging appearance and personality. But wait, I just said you can't see them. The real message is that you can only see them when they want you to. Frequently hikers are stunned when a covey of quail explodes into the air all around them. Bobwhite often allow a close approach, so confident are they that they can remain unseen.

Outside the nesting season Northern Bobwhites become quite bold and confiding. If you scatter cracked corn on the ground, perhaps some of these charmers will visit you.

Bobwhites are about 10 inches from beak to tail and quite round. They look like little chickens, speckled brown and black on most of their bodies with rather short tails. The males have a white throat and a thick white stripe above the eye. Black feathers between these areas tend to set them off. The females have a similar pattern but muted with beiges and browns.

Quail prefer to run rather than fly, and often appear to glide away across the ground like clockwork toys on rapidly moving legs.

One of their most endearing and fascinating behaviors is when they go to roost. They back into a tight circle, like a large doughnut of quail. This is for warmth and also for protection. Observers have described a musical chairs-like process where the last bird in at night runs round and round the circle, looking for a niche to fill before finally jumping atop the group and then walking around until it can wiggle in.

This image also makes me think of the Musk Oxen of the far north who also form a circle facing outwards to fend off marauding wolves. This strategy that worked for hundreds of thousands of years almost caused their extinction when men arrived with guns. It was possible to stand off at a distance and just decimate the herd since they would never actually run away.

Our Northern Bobwhites also fall prey to man and his guns. Indeed this is one of the main features humans seem to love about them – being a game animal. It is a tradition with mid-western farmers to sell shooting rights to sportsmen and thereby pay their annual taxes. Even our Vice-President is known as a semi-successful quail hunter.

Despite all this, Northern Bobwhites have done well by our human intervention. They followed the plow westward as land was cleared. The stubble and grain left over in the autumn provided them with just what they needed to make a living.

But back to that wonderful whistled "Bob – White." This is the male's courting song. Once a girl shows interest an exciting footrace often ensues, both running across the ground with amazing speed. When she makes up her mind, her soft whistled response is a very sweet melody.

The nest of these quail is a sophisticated affair, built of grass on the ground but often with a shield arching overhead. In this nest, anywhere from 12 to 24 eggs may be laid. One nest had 37, but probably had more than one hen laying. After three weeks the chicks hatch and are almost immediately mobile. One was even seen scurrying off with a piece of eggshell on its back. Curiously, their wing feathers develop ahead of the rest of the bird and chicks as young as a week have been seen to fly.

On Nantucket both climate and the sad introduction of feral cats make it impossible for Northern Bobwhites to survive without external assistance. It takes at least half a dozen to form their roosting circles so without a certain critical mass, a cold winter night may kill many.

Right now Northern Bobwhite may be heard calling in the Tom Nevers area and also in 'Sconset. If you are in those areas and hear a whistled "Bob – White" call, try and locate the source. Then wait patiently to see the singer move, and you will observe America's favorite game bird.

June 30 – The Bubbling Cave-diver

If you are visiting here from the mainland, chances are you've been hearing this bird's bubbling song at home since the beginning of May. Alas these energetic, feathered mites are rather uncommon on Nantucket and only recently have we gotten an inkling that they may be nesting.

Both this year and last, island birders have heard its repetitive, joyful toodling from the State Forest. Perhaps there is a nest. But with these frantically busy birds just finding a nest doesn't prove nesting. How's that again?

Just building a nest doesn't mean successful nesting. To be successful a nest must be built, eggs laid, and young birds actually leave the nest to live on their own. These ebullient singers complicate matters by building several nests.

We know this bird as the House Wren, *Troglodytes aedon*. *Troglodytes* means – one who dives into a cave. The second part of the name is for the tragic lady in Greek mythology, Aedon, who mistakenly killed her own son and was transformed into a nightingale by Zeus.

House Wrens are certainly no nightingales but hearing their vivacious song will quicken your heart. The Chippewa Indians of the mid-west called this bird "O-Ju-na-mis-sug-udda-we'-shi," meaning "a big noise for its size."

House Wrens are certainly tiny, less than five inches long. Round and brown, they have only a short tail but make the most of it, frequently cocking it straight up. Almost nondescript, they are the epitome of what birders call "LBJ"s, for "Little Brown Jobs." There is a faint line over the eye and also faint barring under the tail. The girls and boys look identical to us humans. If they weren't so noisy they might easily be missed.

The boys begin singing almost immediately on their return from the south around the end of April. If you are near a House Wren you will hear the song as often as four times a minute, morning to night, through the end of August. They even sing with a mouthful of insects while flying to the feed young. Many report that although initially charming, the refrain becomes a rather annoying nuisance. Roger Tory Peterson describes it as a "choppy gurgling sound, rising in a musical burst, then falling."

Nuisance is as nuisance does. House Wrens are among the most easily annoyed of our feathered friends. Dr. Winsor M. Tyler, a naturalist of the early 1900s comments, "When disturbed, and it takes little to disturb a house wren, the bird bursts forth with a sharp, tense chatter of the Baltimore oriole, or with a long series of nervous fidgety chip-notes."

These wrens have adapted well to living around humans. They are traditionally hole nesters and use bird boxes regularly. To work best for them, the entry hole should be no greater than an inch and a quarter in diameter in order to prevent other birds, like House Sparrows, from entering. The House Sparrow, introduced from Europe in the late 1800s, has greatly reduced House Wren numbers.

Regardless of the actual size of the nest box, House Wrens will endeavor to fill their entire cave with sticks. It's fascinating to watch them thrust amazingly long twigs through the entry hole a little at a time. An entry passageway is fashioned through the tangle that leads to a softly lined resting-place for the six to eight eggs.

House Wrens are often quite opportunistic in choosing a nesting site. In one case, 24 cow skulls had been hung up to bleach and the wrens quickly built nests in 23 of them. Another pair built a nest on the rear axle of an auto which was used daily. When the car went, so did the wrens. Amazingly they successfully hatched their young. Several cases of hollowed-out wasp nests have been noted and, it least in one case,

114

wasps returned the favor by taking over an existing wren house by papering completely over it.

House Wrens also are creative in what they use. Instead of sticks, one nest was constructed completely of nails, tacks, and pieces of wire. Several 'dummy' nests often are constructed, apparently due to excess energy from the males. Or perhaps another motivation appears when he starts in with a second female once the first has started incubating.

House Wren diet is almost totally insects. There are two messages here. One is that if you have these wrens around, they are greatly reducing your insect population. The second is that if you spray insecticide, you will undoubtedly have fewer wrens.

Come September these wrens undergo a personality transformation, becoming shy, retiring and almost silent. So different are they that Audubon decided the House Wrens he found in the autumn were an entirely different species that he called the Wood Wren.

At any rate, they head south where there are still bugs to eat. Only twice has a House Wren hung around Nantucket long enough to be counted on our Christmas Bird Count.

Now is the time to enjoy their vibrant song if you are out walking in the Lover's Lane area. Many migrate past in September through early November but by then they have morphed into Audubon's subtle Wood Wren and are harder to find. *Carpe diem* and *Troglodytes aedon*!

© GCWest

July 7 – Summer Ducks

Summer Ducks? Some aren't! Some say, "if it walks like a duck and it quacks like a duck. Okay it's a duck." Excellent *deduction*!

Summer duck is the nickname given to this shockingly beautiful animal because it nests across most of our country, including the Deep South where there are almost no other ducks in the summertime.

On Nantucket it was considered a very rare bird back in the 50s when I was first learning my birds. This was a great frustration because it was the loveliest duck pictured in my bird guide.

What we're discussing here is the Wood Duck – *Aix sponsa* – that translates to "a duck dressed for a wedding." There is only one other duck in this genus and that is the Mandarin Duck of Southeast Asia, another very fancy looking beast. They are often kept as exotic pets over here and one actually showed up in a back yard on Golf View Drive a few years ago, much to the shock of the owner. Turned out that a local restaurateur had a flock of them for use on the menu and occasionally they'd escape.

Wood Ducks are a distinctly North American Duck, breeding over most of the U.S. except the southwest. When you look at them in your bird book you have the feeling that no bird could actually be this colorful. The head has a shaggy, glossy, dark-green crest that hangs down behind it. There is a white bridle under the chin and a brilliant red ring around the eye. The flanks are a creamy yellow down to the waterline and the throat is a rich mahogany brown. Arthur Cleveland Bent refers to them as the Beau Brummel among ducks. Even the bill has an intricately painted pattern of red, black and white.

Only half the Wood Ducks we see have all this finery. Mrs. Wood Duck has the same shape, but all the colors are washed out, tending towards grays and ecrus. What stands out on her is a white teardrop around the eye. From late July to September the males lose their color as well. Like most waterfowl this is the post-breeding time of eclipse plumage. They molt their feathers in such a way that they become flightless. Their protection is to become just shadows of their former selves and shrink into the background of the swamp, hopefully unnoticed.

Often your first awareness of Wood Ducks will be a strange creaking sound from overhead. It sounds like something in panic and perhaps that's what it reflects as the birds are usually bolting away, the sound traveling rapidly with them. Their white bellies contrast with the darkness of the rest of these ducks whose long rounded tails make them look off-balance.

Wood Ducks are so-named because of their propensity to nest 40 or 50 feet up in trees, often using an abandoned woodpecker hole. The cavity may be as much as three feet deep and the ducklings have a special claw at the end of their little webbed feet that enables them to clamber up to the edge of the hole within a day of hatching. From there they either tumble down into the water or are carried safely by Mom. Then their major hazard is to avoid being eaten by a pickerel or a snapping turtle.

Unfortunately, man is this duck's greatest hazard. The wholesale cutting of our woodlands has made nesting sites hard to come by. This bird is also a favorite hunting target. Originally persecuted for its plumage as well as its taste, population numbers have plummeted over the years, mainly due to habitat loss.

Despite this these ducks are now found regularly on Nantucket, even rarely nesting. Since it is a cavity nester it will use a box. If you travel by the Pout Ponds out on the moors you may notice big bird boxes with large entry holes there.

In the autumn occasionally you will find a Wood Duck feeding with the puddle ducks at Consue Pond off of Union Street. One of my most memorable experiences was with the Sunday morning birders one late fall morning when we saw five or six Wood Ducks land in the red berry bushes on the west side of Miacomet Pond. They sat amongst the branches, looking quite awkward, but nonetheless appearing quite happy as they gorged themselves on the fruit.

A few hang around late into the autumn and even through most of the winter when the weather is mild and the fresh water ponds stay open. We find a small number on most of our Christmas Bird Counts. To see a Summer Duck up close and personal, visit the Edith Andrews bird collection at the Maria Mitchell Natural History Museum at the corner of Milk and Vestal Streets. Call Dr. Bob Kennedy at 228-1782 and someone will be happy to escort you.

In the meantime when you are in the out of doors around Nantucket's ponds listen for that frightened creaking sound overhead. They are always a prized sighting on our island at any time of year.

July 14 – A Sound from the Deep Summer Woods

The whistled call caresses your ear and any tension you feel just evaporates from your body. This is such a relaxing and reassuring sound, most birders are content to just stop and listen for a moment, glad to be hearing it one more season.

The call is a high whistled – "Peeeee – ah – weeeee" – with the last syllable rising. Then often there follows – "Peeeee – ahhhhh" – the last syllable falling. This song is sung slowly, repeated several times a minute through the day.

Another reason this call is such a treat on Nantucket is that we have to wait for it. Long after most of our other nesting birds have arrived, established territory, courted, nested and even fledged their young, this species is still leisurely making its way up the east coast towards us.

Our bird this week is the Eastern Wood-Pewee, a member of the Tyrant Flycatcher family. These are known as 'tyrants' because of the aggressive way in which they defend their nesting territories. Pewees are a sub-group of nine species, including one with the oxymoronic-sounding name "Greater Pewee." But they are named for their calls, not their size.

The Latin name, *Contopus virens,* means 'short-footed' and green, and tells us that the namer, the 18th century Swedish scientist, Linnaeus, had only a dead specimen from which to work. Even the slightest experience with a live pewee would have allowed him to come up with something more meaningful.

So what of this echoing voice from the forest? The singer is a sparrow-sized bird, olive green above and grayish below. There are two white wingbars. You might confuse it with the Eastern Phoebe except for those bars on the wing and the fact that it lacks the tail twitch of that other flycatcher. Only they can tell the boys from the girls. When you see one it is normally perched in a commanding location from which it can sally forth aerobatically to catch insects in flight.

Eastern Wood-Pewees nest from northern Florida up into southern Canada. The pewees out west have been split into their own species but you must hear their call to be sure. But finding their nest – that is the challenge. The nest is a shallow affair on a horizontal limb, typically 20 feet up, trimmed with the same lichen that surrounds it so it looks like another knob on the tree. The three eggs hatch in about two weeks and in about the same period the young are ready to fly. Their 'short' feet are apparently quite strong because attempts to remove them from the nest for study result in their grasping the nest and bringing it along with them.

This species was first found nesting on Nantucket back in 1949. I remember hearing the song almost constantly as I built forts and tree houses in the State Forest back in the 50s. The birds seem scarcer in as this is written, only being reported in the hardwood forests near Squam Swamp.

Perhaps this is indicative of a greater trend. The data from breeding bird censuses over the last decades of the 20th century show a 35% decline in this species. Scientists suggest this is due to habitat loss both in North America and on their wintering grounds in Central and South America. It's also suggested that the increasing White-tailed Deer population may be a factor. The over-browsing of forest undergrowth by these creatures is removing habitat that supports the insects these birds need to live.

The across-the-board reduction in the level of insectivorous birds like this is worrisome. These are our natural controls for those beasties that buzz in our ear and bite at our scalp. With them gone it means people will call for more pesticide use. There are many species in trouble at the top of the food chain and the poisons we are placing in the environment may be the cause.

Now is the time to listen for the haunting "Peeee – ah – weee" calls in Nantucket's woodlands. Squam Swamp is a great place to hear them and also their relatives, the Great Crested Flycatchers.

When fall migration gets going in September and October, this bird becomes more common here but silent. My first introduction was in the pitch pine groves at the west end of the island where they congregate, perching on fence wires and sailing out to catch insects. The sound of their tiny bills snapping as they pursue insects through the air is exciting to hear. These little flycatchers, many only a couple of months old, are stoking up for a 3,000 mile trip, down past Mexico into Central and South America.

With a diet that is 99% insects they are wonderful to have around. By the end of October, they, and the insects, will be gone. Then you'll have to wait until their calls once again echo again from the deep summer woods in June.

July 21 – The Sewing Machine Bird

From the title you might think that this bird would be a Singer – nudge, nudge – wink, wink. But no, it refers to your first thought when seeing this chunky, long-billed sandpiper actively feeding in shallow water. They lean forward, head low, sometimes even submerged, as they probe rapidly up and down, stitching their way across the water.

I originally learned this bird as the Eastern Dowitcher, *Limnodromus griseus,* the gray marsh-runner. Now that species has been split in two – the Short-billed and the Long-billed Dowitcher. This is a rather unfortunate appellation since you can't safely distinguish them by bill length. Most of the dowitchers seen on Nantucket are Short-billed.

Dowitchers are shorebirds. Larger than many of the birds we see scampering in the shallows, they are 10 to 12 inches from beak to tail and it's the variations in that long beak that make most of the difference. There's not much to the tail though, and the feet stick out just a bit beyond it in flight. What you see in flight is a gray, long-billed bird with a white triangular shape going up the back. The short tail has black horizontal bars.

Unfortunately dowitchers are not as common here on Nantucket as they are over on the Cape. Overall, their numbers are still recovering from their enormous persecution about 100 years ago. This was another bird that was shot for food until they were protected by the Migratory Bird Treaty Act of 1918.

When you are fortunate enough to see a flock of dowitchers, note that they fly rather compactly, fine for social interaction, but bad news if a shotgun is aimed at them. In 1840, John James Audubon wrote, "it is not at all uncommon to shoot 20 or 30 of them at once. I have been present when 127 were killed by discharging three barrels." Couple that with the species' dismaying tendency to keep returning in response to the cries of their injured flockmates, and it's amazing there are any dowitchers around for us to see at all.

Perhaps what saved these charming creatures is that their range is quite widespread. Also the fact that they are fairly long-lived, as long as 10 years. So although they were almost hunted out in certain areas, enough survived for them to recover. There are three separate nesting populations, one in the Ungava region of northern Quebec, another from Hudson Bay west through Alberta, and another in southwestern Alaska. It is most likely the Ungava population that migrates past our beaches in April and May.

You might be saying to yourself, "So, we won't find them on Nantucket in the summer." Not true. The Arctic season is so short that the chicks are out of the nest by mid-July and the adult females are already winging their way south. The males finish the parenting duties and follow along in a few weeks.

In the bogs of the boreal forest they lay their four eggs in a simple, grass-lined nest on the ground. Both sexes share incubation duties but once the chicks hatch, Mrs. Dowitcher flies the coop, leaving Daddy to get the kids actually flying. So the first birds arriving in July are adult females. The males and the new crop of youngsters, making their first trip south arrive later. On Nantucket this species becomes common from mid-August until mid-October.

The birds arriving here later in the year are probably from the more western populations. It is those later birds that are more likely to include some of that new species, the Long-billed Dowitcher. But how to tell them apart?

Remember the bill length is generally not useful except in extreme cases. Even Short-billed Dowitchers have fairly long bills. I remember one at the Harbor Flats in December of 2001 whose beak was so long it seemed the bird must fall on its face. In this case, hearing the accelerating "keeks" of the Long-bill instead of the rapid "tu-tu-tu" of the Short-bill as it took off, clinched the identification.

Good places to find Short-billed Dowitchers on Nantucket include the Harbor Flats at low tide, and the 'bathtub' area on Eel Point. Look for them associating with the larger flocks of Least and Semipalmated Sandpipers. Their larger size and sewing machine behavior make them stand out from the rest. Both species of yellowlegs may also be found there but it's easy to separate them by their more deliberate actions, longer necks and shorter bills.

Dowitchers become scarce after the end of October and only one has ever been found as late as the end of December when we do our annual Christmas Bird Count.

124

July 28 – It's a Sandpiper! It's a Thrush!

It's a bird! It's a plane! Well since this is a bird column, odds are this is a bird. This bird acts like a sandpiper, walking while teetering, often along the water's edge. It also has a thrush name. But if you know my columns, you are probably guessing this is neither.

This week's bird has the name "Northern Waterthrush." It does look a bit like a thrush, mainly brown above, black streaks below. It has a heavy white or cream-colored eyebrow. But thrushes are in a different family. This is a member of the wood warbler family. On Nantucket, we may see as many as 37 species of wood warblers each year. The family is known for its bright colored members that are often found high in trees. This bird is an exception.

The noted Massachusetts ornithologist of the early 1900s, Edward Howe Forbush, observed "It is a large wood warbler disguised as a thrush and exhibiting an extreme fondness for water." Dr. Forbush actually carried the title "Economic Ornithologist for the Massachusetts State Board of Agriculture." This must have been a challenge for his business cards, but also speaks to the fact that at the time, every species was evaluated as to whether it was beneficial or detrimental to human society. He also authored the classic three-volume "Birds of Massachusetts (and Other New England States)."

At any rate, when birders see this bird, they often think of the Spotted Sandpiper that behaves in the same manner. It is this behavior that makes both the 'Spotty,' as we like to call them, and the waterthrush, stand out even though their appearance is anything but flashy.

Both these birds walk along with their whole rear end bobbing up and down. It's almost like someone has an invisible string attached and they're continually pulling it. Even when the birds are at rest, the motion continues. The Latin name reflects this motion as well, *Seiurus noveboracensis,* translating to "a tail waver from New York State." The first specimen came from that State.

There are two other 'ground' warblers in this Genus, the Louisiana Waterthrush and the Ovenbird. The Louisiana Waterthrush is considered rare here but a few Ovenbirds pass through each spring, a few more in the fall. Edie Ray had one spend the winter with her last year, a charming addition to her back yard.

Sandpipers and wood warblers are seldom found together, although Spotted Sandpipers are often found away from the shore. Waterthrushes are woodland birds. They like to be on the ground or not more than a few feet above it. They build their nests on or very near the earth in a thicket not far from a swamp or pond.

They nest from southern Canada and down through New England but not near the coast. They have been found to nest as close as Rhode Island and, at high elevations down into Pennsylvania.

It's after nesting that many of them head for our island. They are the harbingers of our fall migration, appearing as soon as late July. On Nantucket your first awareness of a Northern Waterthrush will probably come through your ears. Their call note is very distinctive and rather unbirdlike. It sounds like two heavy metal spikes being clinked together. Roger Tory Peterson describes it as a sharp 'chink.'

From now until mid-October if you are out walking near the little groves of Pitch Pines on the west end of the island you may hear this sound. If you respond with the standard "Spissshhhhing" noise that birders use to whet a bird's curiosity, you may be rewarded with an explosion of brown feathers as a Northern Waterthrush bursts from the underbrush to teeter back and forth on a low limb, regarding you with interest. Later in the season, many of these birds, are hatch-year birds making their first trip south. A few spend the winter in Florida but most head to the Caribbean Islands, or Central and South America. Curiously many winter on the island of Bermuda, a seemingly small target to hit in the midst of so great an ocean.

Waterthrushes may live more than eight years, quite long for a small bird that travels so far over water each year. They have a characteristic known as site fidelity. Summer and winter, they attempt to return to the same exact spot. A bird banded during its autumn flight through Long Island was recovered the following winter in Venezuela and, remarkably, was retrapped a year later at the same place in Venezuela.

Between logging, farming, and homebuilding it seems that every tangle is being replaced by human habitation. Many charming and dainty creatures like these birds are returning from the north or south to find their world is gone.

I hope you get a chance to enjoy a waterthrush over the next few weeks. If you see one, wish it well in hopes it will make its journey south and find its winter home untouched. Then it may be back to see you again at the end of April.

August 4 – Ruddy Turnstone

This bird is a wonderful surprise for beginning birders. It just doesn't have a good public relations person so you don't find it on postage stamps or license plates. Still it quickly becomes one of every birder's favorite birds, both for its appearance and unusual behavior.

Ruddy Turnstones are well-named for that's just what they do, busily scamper around looking under rocks. The name first appeared in the writings of Francis Willoughby, an English ornithologist and ichthyologist, who wrote one of the earliest bird books (in Latin) back in 1676. This species is cosmopolitan, breeding in the Arctic all around the Northern Hemisphere and is found on every continent except Antarctica during migration. Their Latin name, *Arenaria interpres*, translates to the "go-between sandbird," referring to a supposed tendency to alarm other birds when danger approaches.

Roger Tory Peterson describes this bird as "short, robust, and orange-legged." Does that sound like anyone you know? Turnstones are round-ish shorebirds, actually classed as sandpipers. On Nantucket, it is possible to see 30 different species of sandpipers each year. But telling one from another, that's the tough part.

The good news is that the Ruddy Turnstone is almost unmistakable. It has a striking appearance, both on the ground and in the air. One of the things that expands the minds of beginning birders is the pattern a bird shows when it spreads its wings to fly. Intricate and bizarre patterns appear that are not visible except in flight. Their wings and back have a marvelous pattern of black, white, and rusty brown, all sharply delineated, and dramatically contrasting. Five white stripes show vividly, one down the middle of the back and two on each wing. But all this is hidden when the birds are scurrying along the beach.

Turnstones appear quite a different on the ground. The head and chest have an elegant, black and white harlequin pattern. Underneath they are pure white, and the wings and back are a ruddy brown color laced with black. The five white stripes are concealed. The pointed bill seems to turn upward. Watch for the striking orange legs!

The plumage we're describing here is the breeding plumage, the one worn from early spring until August. The good news is that this is the one often seen on Nantucket. At other times of the year the bright colors are muted to brown, but the rest of the patterns remain.

However it is their thoughtful and business-like behavior as they search for food on the beach that fascinates most of us. They amble along, turning over stones and shells. At the wrack line they stick their whole heads into the seaweed, tossing it hither and yon, reminding many observers of pigs rooting for morsels. An old name for them was "horse-foot snipe," because of their feasting on eggs of "horse-foot" crabs. For some reason, we now call these "Horseshoe Crabs," but in thinking about their appearance, "horse-foot" may be better.

Turnstones reside on our island every month except June. During that month almost all of them are in their high Arctic breeding grounds. The birds that pass hurriedly through in May are in northern Greenland in June. There, for a short time, they give up their stone-turning ways and gorge on Scaevola berries.

Their nests are often just a simple depression on the mossy ground, lined with leaves and moss stems. Sometimes they hide their nest in a puffin burrow. They lay four rather large eggs, one per day. An amazing fact is that this three and one half-ounce bird lays a clutch of eggs weighing two thirds as much as they do. Those berries are put to good use! Once the chicks hatch, their main enemies are the predatory gull-like Great Skuas and Arctic Foxes.

As in most shorebirds, the adults depart as soon as the young can find their own food. Several weeks later, as winter approaches, the young turnstones take their first flight south. Some winter as far north as Nantucket, but others head all the way down to Patagonia near the tip of South America. Birds nesting in Alaska make the 2,000-mile flight to the Hawaiian Islands, at least 50 hours in the air, although turnstones are known to light on the water and swim.

The birds that arrive in July and August are mostly adults. Frequently you will see them still in their bright and gaudy breeding plumage. The youngsters that follow sport a feather pattern more like the winter turnstones. After the end of September our Ruddy Turnstones are no longer ruddy and most have departed south. A few hang around, hammering out the barnacles on our jetties. We've had them on all but two of our Christmas Bird Counts, finding over 100 one year. If you see overturned stones on the beach, perhaps a turnstone is not far away!

August 11 – Are you Semipalmated?

I'll let you wonder about that as I tell you other things about this week's bird. Strangely enough, in this 21st century world, I am writing this while whizzing along in the passenger seat of a car headed south through Atlanta, GA. Since our destination is Florida we are rather like the reverse of this shorebird when it is heading north in the spring. They are driven by the need to procreate and perpetuate the species, as they flash along their coastal highway past thousands of other birds that are quite content to stay on Nantucket for the summer. Likewise we zip past similar numbers of local commuters as we head toward our destination 500 miles ahead.

These birds are very similar to the Piping Plovers that spend the summer on our island. Indeed, Pipings are known as the 'dry-sand' plover compared with these shorebirds that birders call the 'wet-sand' plover. Simply enough, Pipings have a sandy white back making them hard to see in dry sand while this species' back is the color of dark brown mud, like we find on mud flats. If they are motionless you can almost step on them before you see them.

Perhaps by now you have guessed this bird is a plover. Right on! It is called the Semipalmated Plover, *Charadrius semipalmatus,* literally 'semi-palmed' referring to the small webs between their toes. A duck foot would be fully palmated. The naturalist who named this species, Charles Lucien Jules Laurent Bonaparte, a nephew of Napoleon and a Prince in his own right, noticed this hint of a web between this bird's toes, different from other plovers. Perhaps it allows them to scamper across soggy mud better than the competition. Certainly they swim better, but not often. There is a Semipalmated Sandpiper as well.

Learning this, beginning birders are a bit stunned, "You mean in addition to trying to figure out leg color on these scurrying little brown jobs, we have to look between their toes as well?" Well, no! Although this fascinated Prince Bonaparte, birding gurus like the late, great Roger Tory Peterson and our current favorite, David Sibley, provide us with other tools. Their dark back, small size, yellow legs, and the single black ring around their neck are good enough. The Killdeer is twice as big and has two rings.

Now back to the flight north – this is a frantic journey. Most all Semipalmated Plovers pass our island in May and are on their breeding grounds from Labrador north, by the second week of June. They are almost continuously on the go, stopping only to feed hurriedly and then be off again.

There they scrape a slight depression in the ground, line it with a few shells and call it their summer home. Three or four eggs are laid and both parents share their care. We can tell this because the males develop a brood patch, an unfeathered area of the belly. This allows them to press their warm skin right on the egg surface to better transfer heat. In most species only the females develop this.

Like their relatives, the Killdeer, they go through a frantic broken wing display to draw attention away from their nest or chicks. After three weeks the precocious chicks hatch and are mobile almost immediately after their downy plumage dries. The Arctic summer is so short and chilly it is no time to hang around naked and helpless like so many birds do for the first few weeks of their life.

Incredibly, their doting parents cut family ties early and some are back on Nantucket's mudflats by early July. Their numbers increase through the month and now the journey is a leisurely one, their critical annual task behind them. About the middle of August, this year's youngsters make their appearance, making their first southward journey.

Although frequently seen with the small sandpipers that we call 'peep,' their behavior immediately distinguishes them. Their flight call, a whistled 'chuweee,' is very distinctive. When watching them, notice that rather than probe into the mud with sharp beaks as the peep do, Semipalmated Plover use their shorter, stubbier beaks to pick food off the surface. The food is all animal-based – worms, small mollusks, various crustaceans, and insects.

These charming and well-marked little plovers are common along Nantucket's shores, particularly the muddy areas, through the middle of October, a few lingering into November. In 2004 one was actually found during the week of our Christmas Bird Count. Some stay in the southeastern U.S. through the winter but most head to more tropical climes before flashing past us on their northward journey in May.

August 18 – Black-winged Redbird – Bird of Mystery?

      If you are interested in birds and have a bird book, this is a bird that whets your appetite for sight. The pictures are so stunning you can't wait to actually experience this bird for yourself. Alas it's not an easy feat. Seeing such intense color spring from your bird book it's hard to imagine these birds can hide, and yet they do so successfully.

      Strangely, non-birders seem to have better luck with them than the rest of us. I hear all to often from wide-eyed friends, "I had a Scarlet Tanager fly across the 'Sconset Road in front of the car!" Or perhaps it would be in their backyard or in the Japonica Bush. Sometimes a heavy rain washes insects from the trees and people observe flocks of tanagers feeding on the lawn. Another story tells about them following a plow, catching the bugs that are stirred up. What an amazing sight this would be but I've never seen it. Yes, this is a bird that almost everyone knows by name and it's an interesting name at that.

Both the word 'tanager' and the Genus name for this bird, *Piranga,* are taken from South American Indian names for these birds. This brings us a subtle message since so many of our bird names originate from Greek or Latin. Like hummingbirds, tanagers are a 'New World' family. There are over 200 species but almost all of them exist exclusively in the tropics.

Many species are 'drop-dead gorgeous' birds, their colors not just painted on, but radiating out from their bodies. People naming them grasp for extraordinary terms, like 'flame-colored,' 'glistening green,' 'crimson-backed,' or 'diademed.' Indeed if you are fortunate enough to see one you immediately get the feeling it must have escaped from an exotic collection because there's no way it should exist here in New England.

To some extent this is a very appropriate feeling. Our tanagers, and we might see three species here on Nantucket, are only in the U.S. in the summer months. During the winter, Central America is not far enough south for them. No, they must head well into South America to mix with other species of their ilk. They are known as 'trans-Gulf' migrants, flying across the Gulf of Mexico rather than taking the land route around.

One lovely May morning a few years ago Nantucket's Sunday morning birders were thrilled to have a male Scarlet Tanager perform for them in a just-budding tree at the Lily Pond. In 50 years of birding this was the best look I've ever gotten and here some of the birders experienced it on their first trip out!

Scarlet Tanagers are smaller than a robin, with jet-black wings and a thick whitish bill. Roger Tory Peterson describes the males as "Flaming scarlet." Female tanagers are hugely different, green above fading to yellow below. And here's the rub for you who are now anticipating going out and seeing this bird. In autumn, all tanagers don these yellow and green colors. For a short time the males are splotched with both red and green, thoroughly confusing a new birder. The species name for this 'black-winged redbird' is *olivacea,* olive-colored, and may indicate that the first specimens were in fall plumage. Also, *Piranga rubra,* the 'red tanager,' had already been used for the Summer Tanager.

For nesting, Scarlet Tanagers choose oak forests. High in these leafy realms they spend their summers, slowly and methodically moving from leaf to leaf, removing every insect they find. Their call note, a striking "chip-burrr," or their rapid song, like a robin with a sore throat, tantalizes birders below. You know they are up there but they are hard to see.

On Nantucket they migrate rapidly through in May, perhaps into early June. Some years we hear them singing in the Hidden Forest and hope they will nest but it's never been proved. In the mainland's hardwood forests they build their simple nests, 20 feet up, and typically well out on a horizontal branch away from the trunk. After the four eggs hatch, the Beau Brummel males quickly lose interest and Mama Tanager finishes raising the next generation.

In August we often observe the red and green males migrating south across our island. In September through mid-October, Scarlet Tanagers are common here but alas, they are all green and yellow and tricky to see. Listen for the "Chip-burrr" call note and then track them down. If you see a tanager in November, it is more likely a bewildered Western Tanager, a very striking Rocky Mountain bird that sometimes migrates east instead of south. They have white wingbars and are easily confused with the young Baltimore Orioles that also hang around into early winter. Birding on Nantucket is never dull.

August 25 – The Bird That Held Back the Tides?

Amazing stories sprout from the study of the most mundane birds. Of course 'mundane' is in the eye of the beholder and many things about this feathered wonder are anything but mundane.

Our bird this week is a shorebird and one of special concern at that. It vies with the Arctic Tern as a long distance traveler, clocking close to 20,000 miles each year, much of this over water.

This bird is nicknamed the 'beach robin,' or 'red-breast," and when you see them in the spring it's easy to understand why. They are robin-sized and sport a lovely rusty red breast. Alas, in autumn when they are most common here, they have molted and replaced their spring finery with a more suitable Nantucket coloration – gray. One writer commented ironically that this bird could be distinguished by its nondescriptness, sounding like a quote from Yogi Berra if he was into multi-syllabic words.

The common name for this bird is the Red Knot. Its Latin name is *Calidris canutus. Calidris* comes from Greek for a gray, speckled sandpiper. Both Knot and *canutus* have a common origin, but naturalists disagree what that is. The simple explanation is they are both onomatopoeic of the bird's call note. But that's a bit boring and not nearly as neat as the other theory.

We trace that back to early English literature where Michael Drayton's Poly-Olbion of 1622 said:

> "The knot was called Canutus bird of old,
> of that great king of Danes,
> his name that still doth hold,
> his appetite to please,
> that farre and neare was sought for him (as some have said),
> from Denmark hither brought."

Here we connect back to this article's title, because one of the legends of King Canute was that he could command the tides. Legends are often confused and confusing. When the Swedish scientist Carolus Linnaeus named this bird of the tidal estuaries, he chose to recognize that myth about the Danish King who at one time ruled England and almost all of Scandinavia in the early 11th century.

This is another species that was fantastically abundant during our early history and then devastated by the draconian hunting methods used in the mid-19th century. Unfortunately some of the worst of this occurred in the Wellfleet area of the outer Cape. The technique was known as 'fire-lighting.' One man would carry a lighted lantern, mesmerizing the birds, and his partner would pick them up, bite them on the neck to dispatch them and then toss them into a sack. Red Knots were considered excellent 'table' birds and commanded the price of 10 cents a dozen. Fortunately this practice was soon prohibited by law, but spring and fall shooting continued into the 1900s and only a pitiful remnant of the original numbers were left. Red Knots have recovered their population largely because this species exists all around the world, and their long migration routes ensure genetic mixing.

On Nantucket the sight of small flocks of these sandpipers arriving on their way north in May, sporting their red breasts, quickens the hearts of our birding community. By early June they are far north in Greenland and the Canadian Arctic for their frantically short nesting season. It takes three weeks for their four eggs, laid in a simple scrape on the ground, to hatch. Both parents incubate and the precocious chicks are instantly mobile as soon as their down has dried. The mothers leave the rest of the parenting to the dads and are the first to head south, arriving back on our island before the end of July, some still sporting their spring duds. They are followed by the adult males, and later, this year's youngsters. Most Red Knots leave us by early October although some hardy ones have hung around to be found on our Christmas Bird Counts.

When we see them in the fall, they are bulked up, ready for a huge migration flight. Many travel over water from our coasts, heading south-southeast to the northern shores of South America, over 3,000 miles. Most don't stop there, heading all the way down to Patagonia at the southern tip of the continent.

Unfortunately Red Knots have dramatically declined over the past 10 years. Although no longer hunted here, they are still commonly hunted in South America (especially the Guianas). Another problem is that this species gravitates to specific staging areas along their migration routes. One particular favorite in spring is Delaware Bay where they feast on the eggs of the horseshoe crab. Humans are now taking many of these horny beasts and grinding them up for use as bait for the eel, whelk, and conch fisheries. So the egg supply is dwindling.

The other dilemma is man's continuing desire to live next to the sea. Marshes and estuaries are under increasing pressure from developers who see billions to be made, building and selling homes for those who can afford them. Less and less room is left for these weary-winged world travelers.

Over the next few weeks, journey to Nantucket's beaches and look for these chunky gray shorebirds, twice the size of the clockwork Sanderlings that chase the waves. Listen for their 'knot' calls in the air and think of the Danish King who tried to hold back the tides.

September 1 – A Whinny from the Swamp

Who knows about rails? Yes they are birds (after all this is a bird column), but have you ever seen one? Amazingly, many people who call themselves birders have not. Hearing them is another story because rails are easily provoked into answering a tape of their calls.

This week's bird is simply known as the Sora. It is one of a very few species known by its Native American name. Another is the towhee. Can you think of any more?

Its Latin name is *Porzana carolina,* and early writings called it the Carolina Rail. *Porzana* means 'crake' in Latin. There is only one species that carries the name crake and that is a European species called the Corn Crake. Its Latin name, *Crex crex*, goes back to a word Aristotle used for a long-legged bird. Our Soras closely resemble this Corn Crake in size and shape.

Soras are roly-poly chicken-like marsh birds. They are close to the length of a robin but have almost no tail. Their length is all body. They are mainly brown with a stubby yellow bill, long yellow legs and huge feet. Adults have black faces fading to gray on the throat.

Now you know what a Sora looks like. Seeing one can take some time and luck. I recall a wonderful afternoon I spent at Edith Andrews' banding table out in Madaket. We had just seen a stunning Rusty Blackbird, fascinating with its pale white eye. Then, lo and behold, here came a Sora ambling through the undergrowth, pecking away at little beasties, seemingly unaware we were 10 feet away. It stepped carefully, gracefully lifting its long yellow toes and then stepping forward, all the time flipping its stubby tail to flash its white underwear.

I've never seen a Sora fly. They much prefer to run away. If you do manage to flush one from the marsh it typically flutters heavily over the tops of the reeds before dropping in again so it can run. Amazingly though, when it's time to migrate they perform with vigor. One of their regular migration stops is Bermuda, a small target for a bird out in the Atlantic. From there they apparently head for South America, a trip of several thousand miles.

Soras nest over much of North America. My first experience with them came 35 years ago, while birding at the Air Force Academy, over 7,000 feet up in Colorado. There, in a small cattail marsh, I heard their whinnying call, much higher than a horse's whinny. It starts as a few uplifting whistles and then is followed by a descending cascade of more rapid ones, almost a trill. It is a delightful and exuberant sound. When I played the call back, I had two Soras come running right up to me, intent on finding this invader.

It doesn't take much of a wet spot to keep a Sora happy. Arthur Cleveland Bent wrote that they could be found on the island of Manhattan until the early 1900s, right next to an active train platform. They still can be seen in Central Park, but only rarely.

The other thing that blows your mind is that these little rails are considered game birds. My first inkling of this came on the island of Taiwan when I encountered a young man creeping through the marsh with a .22 rifle. With my pidgin Chinese I was able to determine he was hunting Moorhens, close cousins to the Sora. Knowing the mainly crustacean diet of these critters, I was amazed to think anyone would eat them. But apparently with enough herbs and spices ...!

In our part of the world they used to be shot in prodigious numbers. In the mid-1800s on Delaware Bay, it was common for each hunter to bring back 100. Here and now, the hunting season runs from September to early November, five per day. If anyone actually goes after them here, I'd love to hear about it.

Soras commonly lay 10 to 12 eggs in a rather elegantly woven nest that sits just above the water in a cattail marsh. There are so many eggs that they rest in two layers, the birds having to shift them regularly to insure they're incubated properly. The chicks are instantly mobile. One observer saw a chick actually come out of the egg, shake itself off and bail out over the side and swim away. Sora chicks are food for snakes, herons, and snapping turtles so laying a dozen eggs each year just keeps things in balance.

On Nantucket Soras are rare through the winter months. They are shy and secretive and we've only found them on four of our Christmas Bird Censuses. Soras are most common in September and October when their ranks are swelled with the season's hatch. So secretive are they that even then, your best chance of seeing one is to go to the bird collection at the Maria Mitchell Association. Four stuffed Soras reside there and you can hold them in your gloved hand and get to know them.

September 8 – Jumbo Shrimp?

This is my favorite oxymoron – akin to 'military intelligence,' or perhaps a Nantucket one, 'wicked good!' This week's bird has the oxymoronic Latin name *Sturnella magna,* the 'large, little starling.' It does sound like the namer was confused.

I remember seeing this bird through my study hall window at Nantucket High, back in the 50s. My class was the first to spend all four years at the new location on Surfside Road. Even back then I was easily distracted by feathered activity and there was a brown bird working its way across the grass outside the window. It was shaped like a starling but too large. It was nervously twitching its tail and when it did that, interesting little white flags showed on either side.

I hadn't seen many Eastern Meadowlarks and never one close up like this. It turned towards me and stood up taller and I was stunned by the combination of bright yellow and black on its throat and breast. This striking sight wiped all thoughts of trying to read about Caesar in Gaul in Latin from my mind.

Meadowlarks are not larks at all. Rather, they are part of the blackbird family. They nest across North America wherever there are hay fields. Typically their neighbors are Red-winged Blackbirds and Bobolinks. I remember finding them around the Bartlett's Farm area in the summertime.

They are known for their spirited whistled song. "Spring of the Year," they whistle, where the word 'year' is high and emphasized. A phone wire is the favorite spot for this activity and the males spend a great part of their day announcing that this is their territory. Out west there is another species, the Western Meadowlark. Its gurgling song is very different but other than that, they are virtually impossible for human observers to distinguish.

Meadowlarks build a domed nest on the ground. The female nestles into the tall grass and artfully weaves a canopy over her. Then many trips are required to bring in the dry grass to form the base. There's an entry on one side, often with a covered passageway leading to it.

Other than singing and defending a territory, Mr. Meadowlark has little to do with family activity. One reason for this is that he may have more than one wife, so his activities involve almost continuous courtship. Roger Tory Peterson comments that the meadowlark call sounds like a 'guttural chatter.' Could this relate to the licentious behavior of the males?

Mama Meadowlark takes as long as two weeks to get the nest built to her satisfaction and spends another two weeks incubating the five eggs. She spends most of her time sitting on her eggs, turning them frequently. Curiously when the male sings high above, she responds with her own subdued song, a sweet series of chuckling notes.

Unlike many ground nesters, Eastern Meadowlark young are not precocious. Blind and helpless at birth, it takes almost two weeks before they are able to move beyond the nest's confines to explore the world. This behavior, along with the exploding feral cat population on Nantucket, may be the main reason we no longer find these 'marsh quail,' as hunters used to call them, nesting on our island.

Another problem for these charming brown, black, and yellow birds is that they favor the sandplain grassland habitat that is falling casualty to man's desire to 'develop' coastal areas. Meadowlark populations have plummeted near the shores and the species has been declared 'of special concern' in Connecticut.

There are still puzzles to be solved. Do meadowlarks migrate by day or night? Some naturalists assert they are nocturnal. Yet, they've been observed migrating across farm fields in a sort of 'leap-frog' manner. The trailing segment of the flock flying to the forefront as they march through a pasture, feeding as they go. Six to eight miles a day can be covered this way.

In any event, they are not serious migrators, only quitting the northern limits of their summer range. Indeed, in recent years, winter is the best season to find them on Nantucket. They have been recorded on almost all of our Christmas Bird Counts although only on about half of the most recent ones. The chart in 'Andrews and Blackshaw' shows them as rare to uncommon most of the year, and completely absent from mid-July until the beginning of September.

The best way to find them now through winter is to visit our remaining sandplain grasslands on the west and south sides of Nantucket. Watch for brown birds flying away, showing a rapid wing-beat followed by a glide on set wings, white flags showing at the sides of the tail. As winter recedes, if you are lucky, you will get to hear their 'spring of the year' announcement.

Birds of the Aleutians – and Nantucket

September 15 – White-winged Scoter

As you are reading this I am on a bird watching trip from Anchorage, Alaska, through the Aleutians, out to Attu Island which is so far to the west it's actually 'east'. The international dateline makes a strange jog to the west just to keep us on the same day. To add to the confusion, Attu is at 173 degrees EAST Longitude, but is still considered the WESTERN-MOST point in the U.S. So this week and next we are looking at two bird species that share this spot with Nantucket, thousands of miles apart.

Our bird is a big, heavy, 'sea' duck abundant on Nantucket Sound in the winter and is just now arriving from the north. It is a traditional favorite with duck hunters who know it as the 'bell coot' because of the interesting ringing noise its wing feathers sometimes make in flight. The common name by which we know it is the White-winged Scoter, *Melanitta fusca,* "a black duck." In Europe and Asia this same species is called the 'Velvet' Scoter, a different species until a few years ago when it was 'lumped' in with the White-winged.

This duck measures the same size as a Mallard but appears larger because of its chunkiness and dark color. The white patch on the trailing edge of the wing is conspicuous in flight in both the drakes and hens but is often concealed when resting. The males are jet black with a white teardrop at the eye, the females browner.

They are just now returning from their nesting homes that range from northern Quebec all the way to Alaska. Interestingly our winter population comes from both locations. In early May it must be confusing as some birds fly off to the west, overland, traveling across the Great Lakes towards central Canada and Alaska, while a much smaller number proceed north through Labrador. There they build a simple nest, often just a depression under a rose bush and lay from nine to 14 eggs. The ducks conceal the eggs under leaves as they depart the nest, making it almost impossible to find.

Except during the nesting season, scoters are almost totally addicted to salt water, so when they arrive here we look for them around our island's shores. Scoters are a common sight here. There are three species often found in the same area. Along with the White-winged there are Surf Scoters, also known as 'Skunkheads', which have big splotches of white on their heads and Black Scoters that have no white on them at all. The females of all three species are browner and can be tricky to separate. At least the White-wings reveal a white wing patch in flight.

Since they live in fairly deep water it comes as no surprise that these birds dive for their food. Intuitively you would guess they are fish eaters but that's incorrect. Most of their diet is mussels and other shellfish that they swallow whole and then either grind up or dissolve internally. What a potent digestive system!

Sea ducks, which include scoters, eiders, and Long-tailed Ducks have always been favorites of sportsman despite their rather poor reputation for flavor. I was amazed as I researched this article how much I read about the joys of getting up in total darkness, rowing boats out into the bay in the chill October winds and then waiting for enough light to be able to see scoters flocking past. The comment is that 15 or 20 birds are considered a good day's 'sport,' although current bag limits are lower. Sea Duck hunting season runs from early October through the end of January, much longer than for other ducks. Nature lovers are often appalled to find that although shooting goes on, there seems little enthusiasm for actually retrieving the birds. 'Sport' is definitely in the eye of the beholder.

Nevertheless, historically, sea duck numbers never seem to suffer. Winter voyages across Nantucket Sound provide wonderful opportunities to see and hear White-winged Scoters doing their thing. Often they are gorged with food and find it difficult to take off. If there is no wind, they must dive to avoid our steamers. With the new 'fast' ferries, some of them aren't quick enough.

When they do take off, you hear the wonderful sound of air rushing through the heavy wing feathers, sometimes with a whistle, sometimes with the bell-like sound that gives 'bell coots' their nickname. Birders love to be out on deck during crossings to enjoy this spectacle. It's free and a wonderful part of island life, on Nantucket and also in the Aleutians.

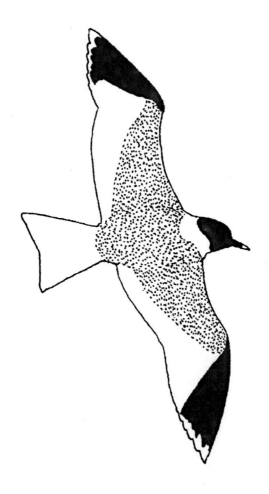

September 22 – The "Unknown" Bird

In case you missed last week's column, I'm now on a birding cruise from Anchorage, Alaska through the Aleutians to Attu Island, so far 'west' it is 'east,' almost in Siberia. I've chosen birds, both this week and last, that may be found in both places.

Our bird this week is a very charming gull whose picture tantalized me for many years. From above, the wing pattern shows five triangles, two black, two white, and one gray. Furthermore, this gull has a forked tail, more characteristic of a tern. It also has a crisp black head, like the Laughing Gulls that used to be more common on Nantucket. If your project was to embellish a Laughing Gull to make it more nifty, a Sabine's Gull could be the result. Even the bill is a cool, black with a yellow tip, similar to a Sandwich Tern. Sandwich Terns are easy to remember since they, "look like their bills are dipped in mayonnaise," as Roger Tory Peterson says.

Sabine's Gulls are not endangered but they are certainly difficult to see. They breed around the world but at very high latitude. We're talking northern Greenland across the Arctic to the Bering Sea and through Arctic Russia across to Spitzbergen Island. When not actually nesting, they are pelagic gulls, usually staying far at sea beyond sight of land, often in the company of Arctic Terns, another global traveler.

The Atlantic birds sweep past us in September and October on their way to the coast of North Africa, and the Pacific birds make a similar journey along the west side of our continent on their way to the Peruvian coast. My only sighting of this bird was a Pacific bird I saw on one of Debbie Shearwater's (yes, she changed her name to this) cruises off Monterrey, California.

So why is this bird 'unknown?' Remarkably, this is its Latin name *Xema sabini*. English naturalist William Leach named this genus, '*Xema*,' meaning literally 'an unknown bird,' perhaps because he was confused by its having both gull and tern characteristics. Sabine's Gull is the only member of this genus.

The eminent scientist, Sir Edward Sabine, collected the first specimen off the coast of Greenland in 1819 while on a voyage with Ross and Perry whose main purpose was to find the legendary Northwest Passage to Asia. Sir Edward is more famous as an astronomer and physicist. His work studying the length of a 'second' pendulum, one that takes a second in each sweep, at varying latitudes, refined the idea that our earth is not a perfect sphere. He also did pioneering and painstaking work studying our planet's magnetic fields. His brother Joseph actually named this gull for Sabine. Joseph, in turn, has one of 10 subspecies of Ruffed Grouse named for him.

Sabine's Gulls lay their three eggs in a very simple ground nest high in the Arctic. Both parents share in the incubation although since the sexes are so similar it's hard to tell who is who. So close are they to the water that occasionally an unusually high tide will wipe out an entire colony. Dr. Edward Nelson, Chief of the U.S. Biological Survey, saw this in Alaska in 1887 and was distressed to note that the gulls had apparently been discouraged from breeding for an entire season by this happening. As with many species that migrate thousands of miles over rough conditions, long life is not to be expected. An eight-year-old Sabine's Gull is hard to find. Losing an annual breeding cycle is serious business.

These gulls are graceful feeders, swooping down and just skimming bits of animal life from the surface, never diving. When feeding on mudflats, they scamper around like sandpipers and with their small size, could be mistaken for plovers.

In the air, their small size, graceful flight, and forked tail make one think of a tern. Indeed this can be a problem since the most likely time to find them around Nantucket is from early September through late October when many terns are migrating through. Also, Sabine's sharply defined black head has faded to gray and white and they are harder to identify.

If you are fortunate enough to go out to the banks east of Nantucket with Captain Blair Perkins on one of his whale-watching cruises, this is a great chance to encounter Sabine's Gull. Others have been seen just off the Jetties after an easterly blow. Watch for the flashy wing-pattern and the wonderful bi-colored bill and perhaps you can add this 'unknown' bird to your life list.

September 29 – Attu and Nantucket Reprise

For those of you just joining us, I just returned from 17 days cruising the Pacific Aleutian Islands, destination Attu at the very end. The preceding two columns were about birds I figured I would find up there that were also Nantucketers. One of them worked out. The other we missed.

In the first week I told you all about White-winged Scoters. I saw a few up there but they were scarce. The second week's was a major disappointment – Sabine's Gull. It was an expected bird but none showed up. Darned birds anyway – flighty things! But I did find three Nantucket birds on the island of Attu, and land birds at that.

I'll let you try and guess what they are while I describe this island at the end of nowhere. It is 35 by 20 miles and very mountainous, old volcanoes up to 2500 feet high. There are absolutely no trees other than the three pathetic firs planted by some Navy folk 50 years ago. Right now there are only 20 inhabitants, all Coastguardsmen, who maintain a big LORAN antenna exactly like the one we have on the east end of Nantucket. Originally there were native Aleuts but they were relocated at the beginning of World War II, never to return.

The weather is mostly rainy, foggy and windy. There were 80 knot winds the week before we arrived. You can expect only eight or 10 sunny days per year! We were blessed with six gorgeous sunny days on Attu so there goes most of the quota. It pays to choose the right tour company.

So now you have the comparison in mind – one island, 15 by 3 miles, quite wooded, max elevation 100 feet – and the other, about twice the size of the Vineyard, but with high mountains and no trees. What birds could we share?

It turns out the most common between us is the good ol' Song Sparrow, *Melospiza melodia.* These brown, stripy, LBJs (Little Brown Jobs) are our year 'round friends here on Nantucket. Interestingly, this species is one of the most widely distributed North American birds with 31 subspecies, or local variants. Subspecies carry a third Latin name after the first two. The race on Attu is known as *maxima,* and it is a 'giant' Song Sparrow. In cold climates, the larger you are, the more efficient you are at retaining heat. So being a big Song Sparrow is a good thing if you live in such an inhospitable climate.

The bird I visited with on Attu was almost unrecognizable as a Song Sparrow, until it opened its beak that is. If you know Song Sparrows, what they absolutely can not do is keep silent. References describe the Song Sparrow call note as 'tchenk,' 'tchip,' 'tchunk,' 'chip,' 'tcheek,' or 'chuck.' I tend to lean toward 'tchunk' myself and when this large, very dark bird uttered that sound, I knew I had found an old friend.

These big, dark sparrows are one of the few avian year 'round residents on Attu. They mainly inhabit the coastal areas and I would see them out, hopping around the kelp with the Rock Sandpipers and the Pacific Golden Plover. In the wintertime, these are the only areas not deeply covered in snow so this type of adaptation is a requirement for survival.

The second bird was easily the most ubiquitous species with which we had to contend. Indeed, they were in the air around us almost constantly and their calls always in our ears. We had to be careful not to miss a rare Asian species because of all this noise.

On Nantucket this is a great bird to find – a rarity on our beaches from now through early April. Its name is the Lapland Longspur, *Calcarius lapponicus,* a direct translation of its English name. Longspurs have an extraordinarily long hind claw and the first specimen came from northern Scandinavia.

They are another sparrow-sized LBJ and the last time I enjoyed them on Nantucket was out near the LORAN antenna at Low Beach one winter day as they fraternized with the more common Snow Buntings.

On Attu they were gathering in larger and larger flocks, getting ready to migrate south. Some would head down to Japan, others over to Alaska and British Columbia. One wonders how they choose.

The final bird I'll mention is the Winter Wren. All across Europe and Asia it is the only wren so there it is just known as the Wren. This is yet another LBJ, only this one is smaller and browner than the rest. It has almost no tail and is quite mouse-like in its behavior, often running away under things rather than flying.

Perhaps the Attu birds were mainly youngsters because they came easily to a 'spishhhing' noise and skulked much less than the ones we find on Nantucket. Here they are just arriving and can be found all winter. In the springtime, the lucky birders who still have good high frequency hearing can thrill to the long, cascading, tinkling song these feathered marvels can produce.

As you can no doubt tell, my body is back on Nantucket but my brain is still somewhere in between. I hope you've enjoyed flashing around the world with me this week.

154

Afterword

This completes Volume Three and a third year of birding Nantucket. As I write this I already writing Volume Five as my weekly columns in The Nantucket Independent continue to accumulate.

A reader commented to me that at the end of Volume One I left you with little flycatchers launching themselves out over the Atlantic from our southwestern shores, most to a watery grave. This seemed a bit of a downer.

That reader was certainly correct. Nature often seems cruel in its ways. So often we are left in great pain when creatures we love and enjoy succumb before our eyes.

Another friend asked what to do about a Merlin that was killing the birds at his feeders. Tough question! My answer has to be "Nothing." We hate to see a Mourning Dove as a meal, but having another bird starve to death is terrible as well.

So every birding year has its ups and downs. A story is told of bird life on our island that continues on relentlessly regardless of human interference or support.

This volume ends with me just having returned from a birder's dream experience, a trip to Attu Island, 1500 miles west of Anchorage, almost in Russia. We thought our days of being able to visit this lonely island were gone when Attour stopped doing business in 2000. Victor Emanuel brought these dreams back to life by chartering a whole cruise ship so that 100 birders could do Attu in style.

So island birding adventures continue. Nantucket is not Attu but it is still unique and exciting from a birder's perspective. As I said earlier, if you enjoyed Volume Three, don't hesitate to pick up Volumes One and Two as well. You can travel to exotic places and learn about our marvelous avian companions without leaving your easy chair.

About the Artist

George C. West started birding and drawing birds in Newton, Massachusetts when a 4th grade teacher sparked his interest in birds. Drawing and painting birds since 1940, he has illustrated many publications and contributed illustrations to many non-profit ecological and ornithological agencies as well as offering his art for sale to the public.

He has a Ph.D. from the University of Illinois, was awarded a postdoctoral fellowship at the National Research Council of Canada and an Alexander von Humbolt fellowship at the Max Planck Institute for Behavioral Physiology in Germany. He taught at the University of Rhode Island and helped form the Institute of Arctic Biology at the University of Alaska Fairbanks where he spent 21 years conducting field and laboratory research on arctic and subarctic birds, mammals, plants, ecosystems, and training graduate students. After a stint as Director of the Institute, he ended his academic career as Vice President for Academic Affairs of the University of Alaska Statewide System before retiring in 1984 as Professor of Zoophysiology, Emeritus.

He has published over 90 scientific articles and books. He and his wife, Ellen spent the next 12 years on the shores of Kachemak Bay in Homer, Alaska, where Partners in Flight awarded him for increasing public awareness of the need for habitat conservation for migrating shorebirds. He is the author and illustrator of the American Birding Association's *A Birders Guide to Alaska*. In 1996 he and Ellen moved to Green Valley, Arizona where he has continued birding, illustrating birding publications, and co-founded the Hummingbird Monitoring Network. He is preparing an illustrated guide to North American Hummingbirds.

Other Nantucket Birding Publications

by Kenneth Turner Blackshaw

A Year of Birding Nantucket: Volume One,

A Year of Birding Nantucket: Volume Two

Birding Nantucket (with Edith F. Andrews)

Bike Birding Nantucket

All of these books are available at all bookstores on Nantucket Island. The first three are also available through Amazon.com.